RELEVANT KNOWLEDGE SERIES

EMPIRICAL GENERALIZATIONS

ABOUT

MARKETING IMPACT

EDITED BY
DOMINIQUE M. HANSSENS

Copyright 2015 Marketing Science Institute
Published by Marketing Science Institute, 1000 Massachusetts Ave., Cambridge MA 02138
ISBN-13 978-0-9823877-3-3
All rights reserved. No part of this book may be reproduced, in any form or by any means, electronic or mechanical, without permission in writing from the Institute and the author.

Cover design by Ryan Ratliff, RR Web & Print

Contents

Foreword	1
Introduction	3
Glossary	5
1: Marketing Orientation and Market Structure	7
2: Effects of Economic Cycles	19
3: Customer Satisfaction and Product Reviews	29
4: Objective and Perceived Quality	41
5: Market Share	47
6: Order of Entry	57
7: Sales Diffusion and Social Influence	67
8: Product Innovation	85
9: Price Effects	103
10: Brands and Brand Loyalty	117
11: Price Promotions	129
12: Personal Selling	139
13: Distribution	143
14: Advertising	153
15: Marketing Mix	179
16: Competitive Reaction	191
About the Editor	193
About the Marketing Science Institute	195

Foreword

When the Marketing Science Institute was founded, very little sound research was available to aid managers in decision making. Since then, thousands of articles, books, etc. have been written. However, accessible syntheses of this work are few and far between. For that reason, in 2002 MSI launched the Relevant Knowledge Series, a collection of short monographs that summarized and interpreted academic research in areas related to MSI's research priorities (e.g., new product adoption, pricing, metrics, and branding).

In 2009, Mike Hanssens came up with an interesting variation. Rather than providing a modestly comprehensive overview of a single area, he compiled a series of brief "empirical generalizations" across a broad range of topics. These generalizations (often based on meta-analyses) basically summarize the quantitative knowledge that has been accumulated in academic research. This hits a "sweet spot" by providing "top-line" information useful in, among other things, setting and evaluating budgets. For example, because typically a 20% increase in ad spending produces less than a 1% increase in sales, then a budget built on the premise that a 20% increase in ad spending will increase sales 10% is open to questions such as "what makes your advertising so special?" More broadly, empirical generalizations are both a (if not *the*) goal of academic research and a way to make sense of the explosion of research which is now widely available (analogous to the problem of dealing with big data).

This volume is the updated version of that effort. It succinctly summarizes basic results in 16 areas. We believe there is something (actually, multiple "somethings") in this for everyone.

Donald R. Lehmann
Columbia University
MSI Executive Director 1993–95, 2001–03

Introduction

The purpose of the first edition of *Empirical Generalizations about Marketing Impact*, published in 2009, was to disseminate the generalized findings that have emerged in academic research on the impact of marketing activity on firm performance.

The 2009 book has been very well-received. It has become the best seller in MSI's Relevant Knowledge Series, it was designated a "Must Read" by *Quirk's Marketing Research Review* in 2013, and it is being used by academics and marketing practitioners alike.

Furthermore, in 2011, Joseph Alba of the University of Florida followed up on this initiative by editing a collection of empirical generalizations on consumer behavior, *Consumer Insights: Findings from Behavioral Research*. Taken together, the two books provide concise and accessible summaries of what rigorous academic research has contributed to these two important pillars of the marketing discipline.

The positive response to *Empirical Generalizations about Marketing Impact* has motivated me to edit an updated and expanded version. As with the first edition, I obtained a virtually perfect response rate to my request to authors to update their 2009 empirical generalizations and/or provide new contributions. The result is that the 2015 version of the book has about 50% more empirical generalizations, now totaling 123. In particular, our discipline has gained several new insights due to the presence of high-quality digital marketing databases. My sincere thanks to these authors for generously contributing their time and expertise.

As the following entries demonstrate, replicable patterns in marketing exist and can often be quantified so that managers have access to benchmarks of marketing impact. At the same time, developing and testing these benchmarks is a work in progress. Some empirical generalizations will benefit from a sharper quantification, or replication in other sectors or regional markets, or additional contingencies. Further, generalizations on strategic topics tend to be less precise than those on tactical aspects of marketing. It is my hope that the gaps in our knowledge will serve as a catalyst for new research on marketing generalizations, for the benefit of marketing practitioners and marketing researchers alike.

Dominique M. Hanssens

Glossary

The following metrics and statistics are frequently used in the empirical generalizations. They are generally obtained either by statistical analysis of historical data or by controlled experiments.

Coefficient of variation: the standard deviation of a variable, divided by its mean.

Correlation (r): a measure of linear association between two variables X and Y, ranging between −1 and +1. The higher the correlation in absolute value, the more tightly the two variables co-move with each other. Correlation measures linear association, but does not establish the direction of causality between X and Y.

Diffusion of innovation: the **coefficient of innovation (p)** is the fraction of first purchasers who are innovators in the sense that they are not influenced by other buyers. For example, $p = .02$ means that 2% of the eventual adopters of a new durable product or service are innovators (and therefore 2% of total adoption sales are realized in the first period).

Diffusion of innovation: the **coefficient of imitation (q)** reflects the speed of imitation among first purchasers of a new durable product or service. The higher the value q, the stronger the influence of previous buyers on future buyers, through word-of-mouth and network effects. For a new product to be commercially successful, $q > p$, but if q is only marginally greater than p, diffusion will be slow and protracted. The ratio q/p measures the degree to which the S shape is pronounced.

E-score is measured as the [(# of observations with a significant positive effect − # of observations with a significant negative effect)/ Total # of observations].

Fisher z-score is the [sum of z-scores of individual effect observations/ square root of total effect observations].

Elasticity: a measure of the relative impact of a change in a variable X on another variable Y, defined as percent change in Y divided by percent change in X. For example, an advertising-to-sales elasticity of .08 means that, all else equal, an increase in advertising spending of 10% results in a sales increase of .8%. Elasticity implies a causal direction.

Eta (η), or the correlation ratio between X and Y, is the square root of the proportion of the variance of Y accounted for by X.

Gini coefficient: a measure of income inequality in a country, scaled between 0 and 1. The lower the Gini coefficient, the more equal the income distribution, and vice versa.

Hofstede culture assessment: a five-dimensional scale that measures a country or culture's orientation toward individualism/collectivism, high/low power distance, masculinity/femininity, uncertainty avoidance and long- vs. short-term orientation.

1
Marketing Orientation and Market Structure

Marketing Capabilities

The linear relationship between marketing capability and firm performance is positive ($r = .35$) and stronger than those for R&D ($r = .28$) or operations ($r = .21$) capabilities.

Evidence base	114 studies reporting 786 effect sizes
Managerial implications	Increase in marketing capability is associated with stronger improvement in firm performance than increases in operations capability and R&D capability.
Contributors	Alexander Krasnikov, George Washington University, and Satish Jayachandran, University of South Carolina
Reference	Krasnikov, Alexander, and Satish Jayachandran (2008), "The Relative Impact of Marketing, Research-and-Development, and Operations Capabilities on Firm Performance." *Journal of Marketing* 72 (4), 1–11

Service Transition Strategy

Service transition strategies, i.e., moving from a product- to a service-centric business, add to shareholder value. However, the positive impact of service transition strategies only starts to affect shareholder value when the firm reaches a critical mass of services sales of 20–30%, at which point they have an increasingly positive effect.

Evidence base	477 publicly traded U.S. manufacturing firms from 1990 to 2005
Managerial implications	Service transition strategies may fail to generate shareholder value if the push into services is half-hearted. Companies should recognize that service transition strategies typically require building a critical mass in sales of services-to-products ratio in the product/service portfolio, estimated to be 20–30%, before they can expect positive effects on shareholder value.
Contributor	Jan-Benedict E.M. Steenkamp, University of North Carolina at Chapel Hill
Reference	Fang, Eric, Robert W. Palmatier, and Jan-Benedict E.M. Steenkamp (2008), "Effect of Service Transition Strategies on Firm Value." *Journal of Marketing* 72 (5), 1–14

Impact of Market Orientation

Market orientation (i.e., the organizational activities related to the generation and dissemination of and responsiveness to market intelligence, as well as the organizational norms and values that encourage behaviors consistent with market orientation) has a positive effect on organizational performance ($r = .32$), as measured by profits, sales, and market share. The market orientation–performance correlation is higher in manufacturing businesses ($r = .37$), compared to service businesses ($r = .26$). The association is stronger in countries that are low rather than high on power distance (i.e., how society deals with the fact that people are unequal in physical and intellectual capabilities) ($r = .33$ versus $r = .27$) and uncertainty avoidance (i.e., the extent to which a culture socializes its members into accepting ambiguous situations and tolerating uncertainty) ($r = .34$ versus $r = .27$).

Evidence base	Meta-analysis of 114 prior studies
Managerial implications	Market orientation provides a competitive advantage that leads to superior organizational performance. Even though the implementation of market orientation demands resources, it generates profits over and above the costs involved in its implementation, while concurrently growing revenues. This impact is greater in manufacturing businesses than in service industries. The implementation of market orientation processes should be adapted to local cultural sensitivities.
Contributors	William O. Bearden, University of South Carolina, Satish Jayachandran, University of South Carolina, and Ahmet H. Kirca, Michigan State University

Reference   Kirca, Ahmet H., Satish Jayachandran, and William O. Bearden (2005), "Market Orientation: A Meta-Analytic Review and Assessment of Its Antecedents and Impact on Performance." *Journal of Marketing* 69 (2), 24–41

Drivers of Market Orientation

While interdepartmental connectedness (i.e., the degree of formal and informal contact among employees across departments) has the strongest impact on market orientation ($r = .56$), top management emphasis (i.e., top management reinforcement of the importance of a market orientation) ($r = .44$) and market-based reward systems (i.e., reliance on market-based factors, such as customer satisfaction, for evaluating and rewarding managers and employees in organizations) ($r = .41$) also positively affect a firm's market orientation.

Evidence base	Meta-analysis of 114 prior studies
Managerial implications	By ensuring top management emphasis, interdepartmental connectedness, and customer-satisfaction-based reward systems, market orientation can be effectively implemented in organizations.
Contributors	William O. Bearden, University of South Carolina, Satish Jayachandran, University of South Carolina, and Ahmet H. Kirca, Michigan State University
Reference	Kirca, Ahmet H., Satish Jayachandran, and William O. Bearden (2005), "Market Orientation: A Meta-Analytic Review and Assessment of Its Antecedents and Impact on Performance." *Journal of Marketing* 69 (2), 24–41

Customer Centricity and Performance

A customer-centric structure—an organizational design that aligns each business unit with a distinct customer group (versus product group)—increases customer satisfaction but degrades performance by adding to coordinating costs. Analyses on the 420 firms from the Fortune 500 reveal that the average overall performance for customer-centric firms relative to product-centric firms varies from +10% to −23%, depending on the environment (i.e., competitors' customer-centric structure, industry competitiveness, industry profitability). That is, the benefits of customer-centric structure diminish as (1) competitors' customer-centric structure increases, (2) industry competition intensifies, and (3) industry profitability decreases.

Evidence base	Analyses of 13 years of organizational structure data covering 420 firms from the Fortune 500
Managerial implications	Neglecting the trade-offs in customer-centric structures can create misguided managerial expectations about the returns from restructuring. The ultimate impact of a customer-centric structure on performance likely depends on whether the customer-centric benefits (e.g., customization, responsiveness) outweigh the additional costs (e.g., economic inefficiency and complex coordination).
	Managers should evaluate their competitive environment (e.g., competitor's structure, competitiveness, industry profitability) to understand if shifting to a customer-centric structure is appropriate for them.
Contributors	Ju-Yeon Lee, Lehigh University, Shrihari Sridhar, Pennsylvania State University, and Robert W. Palmatier, University of Washington

References

Lee, Ju-Yeon, Irina V. Kozlenkova, and Robert W. Palmatier (2015), "Structural Marketing: Using Organizational Structure to Achieve Marketing Objectives." *Journal of the Academy of Marketing Science* 43 (1), 73–99

Lee, Ju-Yeon, Shrihari Sridhar, Conor M. Henderson, and Robert W. Palmatier (2015), "Effect of Customer-Centric Structure on Long-Term Financial Performance." *Marketing Science* 34 (2), 250–68

Organic Sales Growth: Internal Drivers

Entrepreneurial orientation (elasticity 1.13), management capacity (.7), innovation (.6), advertising (.38), inter-organizational networks (.26), and firm size (.2) have a positive impact on sales growth. Firm age has a negative impact (−.96).

Evidence base	Meta-analysis of 19 major business academic journals for the period 1960–2008. The number of individual elasticities used to calculate the effect size above varies from 339 for firm size to 57 for entrepreneurial orientation.
Managerial implications	In terms of investments/spending of firms, innovation has the greatest positive impact on sales growth. Similarly, advertising has a positive impact. Thus, managers should think about innovation in tandem with advertising. Value creation (through innovation) needs to be capitalized by means of value communication (through advertising) in order to generate organic growth (sales growth).
	It is important for managers to create an entrepreneurial environment in their firms. Entrepreneurial orientation is likely to influence the intensity and quality of innovation and marketing processes. For example, entrepreneurial behavior in a firm can trigger the development of new product proposals which would increase firms' odds of identifying growth options.
Contributors	S. Cem Bahadir, Özyeğin University, and Sundar Bharadwaj, University of Georgia
Reference	Bahadir, S. Cem, Sundar Bharadwaj, and Michael Parzen (2009), "A Meta-Analysis of the Determinants of Organic Sales Growth." *International Journal of Research in Marketing* 26 (4), 263–75

Organic Sales Growth: External Drivers

Market dynamism (elasticity −.61) and competition (−.05) have a negative impact on organic sales growth. Munificence has a positive impact (.06).

Evidence base	Meta-analysis of 19 major business academic journals for the period 1960–2008. The number of individual elasticities used to calculate the effect size above varies from 104 for competition to 63 for dynamism.
Managerial implications	The results suggest that firms should select non-dynamic and munificent industry environments in which to compete in order to maximize organic growth. In other words, managers need to consider market dynamism (e.g., how fast consumer preferences change) and munificence of the environment (e.g., availability of resources) along with competitive intensity in market-entry decisions.
Contributors	S. Cem Bahadir, Özyeğin University, and Sundar Bharadwaj, University of Georgia
Reference	Bahadir, S. Cem, Sundar Bharadwaj, and Michael Parzen (2009), "A Meta-Analysis of the Determinants of Organic Sales Growth." *International Journal of Research in Marketing* 26 (4), 263–75

The Rule of Three: Market Structure and Performance

Mature and competitive markets tend to converge to a structure with exactly three large firms (generalists) and numerous small firms (specialists). Markets with more or fewer than three dominant players underperform those with exactly three dominant players. For example, firms in conforming industries had an average operating ROA of 15% in 2002, whereas industries with fewer or more than three generalists averaged only 5% and 7% respectively.

Evidence base	Examination of average ROA, ROS, cumulative abnormal stock market returns (CAR), and absolute and relative market share of over 150 U.S. markets in two time periods
Managerial implications	The number of dominant players is an indicator of market attractiveness and evolution. Fewer than three generalists imply a growth opportunity for a third player, whereas more than three implies excessive competition. Both scenarios have strategy implications for organic growth, M&A, and spin-offs. Generalists benefit from converging to and maintaining the "rule of three" structure.
Contributor	Can Uslay, Rutgers University
References	Sheth, Jagdish N., and Rajendra S. Sisodia (2002), *The Rule of Three: Surviving and Thriving in Competitive Markets*. New York, N.Y.: The Free Press
	Uslay, Can, Z. Ayca Altintig, and Robert D. Winsor (2010), "An Empirical Examination of the 'Rule of Three': Strategy Implications for Top Management, Marketers, and Investors." *Journal of Marketing* 74 (2), 20–39

The Rule of Three: Market Share and Performance

Market share and financial performance are related in a non-linear, skewed-U fashion. Both large share (generalists) and smaller firms (specialists) tend to perform better than those stuck in the middle. Excessively dominant players underperform as well.

For example, the generalists' operating ROA for the firms in the 1997 sample was 11% and the specialists fared even better with 14%, but those stuck in the middle averaged 6%. The performance penalty for being stuck in the middle can exceed −50%.

Evidence base	Examination of average ROA, ROS, cumulative abnormal stock market returns (CAR), and absolute and relative market share of over 150 U.S. markets in two time periods
Managerial implications	Firms should steer away from the financial "ditch" of 5–10% market share. Both specialists that have outgrown their niche and undersized generalists lacking economies of scale and scope may find themselves stuck in the middle. These firms may then become M&A candidates when they underperform. Ditch-exit strategies include organic growth, M&A, and downsizing. Firms approaching market dominance are better off growing in other markets due to diminishing returns to market share.
Contributor	Can Uslay, Rutgers University
References	Sheth, Jagdish N., and Rajendra S. Sisodia (2002), *The Rule of Three: Surviving and Thriving in Competitive Markets*. New York, N.Y.: The Free Press

Uslay, Can, Z. Ayca Altintig, and Robert D. Winsor (2010), "An Empirical Examination of the 'Rule of Three': Strategy Implications for Top Management, Marketers, and Investors." *Journal of Marketing* 74 (2), 20–39

2

Effects of Economic Cycles

Consumer Durables and Business Cycles

Consumer durables are more sensitive to business-cycle fluctuations than most other sectors in the economy. The average cyclical volatility (measured as the standard deviation of the cyclical component in the series, which is obtained after filtering out the very short- and long-run fluctuations in the series) is more than four times that of GNP's cyclical component, and the average co-movement elasticity (expressing the extent to which cyclical fluctuations in the economy are translated into cyclical fluctuations in the series of interest) is larger than two.

Evidence base	Diffusion of 24 consumer durables in the U.S. over multiple decades
Managerial implications	Managers should explicitly consider the cyclical variation in the sales of durable products, especially since the extent of this sensitivity can be moderated through the products' pricing strategy. This sensitivity is asymmetric across expansions and contractions, as durable sales fall more quickly during contractions than they recover during economic expansions.
Contributors	Barbara Deleersnyder, Tilburg University, and Marnik G. Dekimpe, Tilburg University and Catholic University of Leuven

Reference   Deleersnyder, Barbara, Marnik G. Dekimpe, Miklos Sarvary, and Philip M. Parker (2004), "Weathering Tight Economic Times: The Sales Evolution of Consumer Durables over the Business Cycle." *Quantitative Marketing and Economics* 2 (4), 347–83

Advertising and Business Cycles

Advertising is more sensitive to business-cycle fluctuations than the economy as a whole, with an average co-movement elasticity of 1.4. Hence, a 1% increase (reduction) in the cyclical component of GDP (obtained after filtering out both the very short-run fluctuations and the long-run trend) translates, on average, into a 1.4% increase (reduction) in the cyclical component of the demand for advertising. The extent of this sensitivity varies systematically across countries depending on cultural and socio-economic factors. When companies tie their advertising spending too tightly to business cycles, managerial and social losses are incurred. These losses extend far beyond the recession period, and are reflected in (1) a lower long-term growth of the advertising industry, (2) a higher private label share, and (3) lower stock prices.

Evidence base	Advertising spending in 37 countries, across all continents, covering up to 25 years and four media: magazines, newspapers, radio, and television
Managerial implications	Countries where advertising spending behaves more cyclically exhibit slower growth of the advertising industry and higher private label growth. Stock-price performance is lower for companies that exhibit stronger pro-cyclical spending patterns. Systematic differences in cyclical sensitivity across both countries and media offer risk diversification opportunities.
Contributors	Barbara Deleersnyder, Tilburg University, Marnik G. Dekimpe, Tilburg University and Catholic University of Leuven, and Jan-Benedict E.M. Steenkamp, University of North Carolina at Chapel Hill

Reference Deleersnyder, Barbara, Marnik G. Dekimpe, Jan-Benedict E.M. Steenkamp, and Peter S.H. Leeflang (2009), "The Role of National Culture in Advertising's Sensitivity to Business Cycles: An Investigation across Continents." *Journal of Marketing Research* 46 (5), 623–36

Private Label Share and Business Cycles

Private label share behaves countercyclically. A 1% reduction in the cyclical component of GDP per capita translates into an increase of .96% in the cyclical component of private label share, and vice versa. Moreover, consumers switch more extensively to store brands during recessions than they switch back to national brands in a subsequent recovery. Finally, a substantial fraction keeps on buying the private labels even when bad economic times are long over. Specifically, when GDP per capita decreases 1% compared to the peak just before the contraction, a long-run upward lift in private label growth of 1.22% occurs. This is attributed to a temporary acceleration in the growth rate of private labels during contractions. In particular, during an expansion, average yearly long-run growth of private label share in the U.S. is 2.26%, but this growth rate accelerates to 7.65% during contraction periods.

Evidence base	Evolution of private label share over multiple decades in the U.S., Germany, Belgium, and the U.K., and evolution in private label share over two decades across 106 consumer packaged goods categories in the U.S.
Managerial implications	Many consumers switch to private labels during an economic contraction, but not all of them switch back to national brands when the economy improves again. Hence, economic recessions contribute to the prolonged upward evolution in private label share. While business cycle fluctuations are beyond the control of individual managers, the dominant practice of reducing brand support during bad economic times reinforces the success of private labels during recessions and afterwards. Manufacturers are able to mitigate the impact of an economic downturn on

their brands' position by engaging in "proactive marketing," i.e., adopt a strategy in which they invest aggressively in major new product introductions, advertising, and promotions during the recession, while the price gap between national brands and private labels needs to be reduced temporarily. Such a strategy is not often observed in the market.

Contributors Barbara Deleersnyder, Tilburg University, Marnik G. Dekimpe, Tilburg University and Catholic University of Leuven, and Jan-Benedict E.M. Steenkamp, University of North Carolina at Chapel Hill

References Lamey, Lien, Barbara Deleersnyder, Marnik G. Dekimpe, and Jan-Benedict E.M. Steenkamp (2007), "How Business Cycles Contribute to Private-Label Success: Evidence from the United States and Europe." *Journal of Marketing* 71 (1), 1–15

Lamey, Lien, Barbara Deleersnyder, Jan-Benedict E.M. Steenkamp, and Marnik G. Dekimpe (2012), "The Effect of Business-Cycle Fluctuations on Private-Label Share: What Has Marketing Conduct Got to Do With It?" *Journal of Marketing* 76 (1), 1–19

Price Elasticity and Economic Growth

On average, consumer price sensitivity is countercyclical—it rises when the macroeconomy weakens. However, substantial variation exists: countercyclical categories tend to be less elastic (e.g., yogurt at −1.7), whereas procyclical categories are relatively more elastic (e.g., deodorant at −2.9). Independent of a category's elasticity, countercyclical categories are those that command a higher share-of-wallet.

Evidence base	Analysis of household-level panel data from 19 categories, spanning six years and over 1.8 million purchases
Managerial implications	Blanket claims that consumer price sensitivity rises during recessions are incorrect. Instead of reacting to the economic climate, managers should study how consumers react to pricing in particular categories. Consumer price sensitivity increases during recessions in categories that comprise a significant share of consumers' budgets.
Contributors	Brett Gordon, Northwestern University, Avi Goldfarb, University of Toronto, and Yang Li, Cheung Kong Graduate School of Business
Reference	Gordon, Brett R., Avi Goldfarb, and Yang Li (2013), "Does Price Elasticity Vary with Economic Growth? A Cross-Category Analysis." *Journal of Marketing Research* 50 (1), 4–23

Price and Advertising Effectiveness over the Business Cycle

In consumer packaged goods, long-term price sensitivity increases during economic downturns. Conversely, the long-term advertising sensitivity (elasticity) is significantly smaller compared to upturns. Comparing the expansion period just prior to the 2009 global financial crisis to the downturn during this crisis, the average long-term price sensitivity increased by 14% (the elasticity went from −.79 to −.90), whereas the advertising elasticities dropped by 60% (from .022 to .009). The short-run price and advertising elasticities are not affected by the business cycle.

Evidence base	Advertising and price elasticities for 150 brands across 36 consumer packaged goods categories, using 18 years of monthly U.K. data from 1993 to 2010
Managerial implications	For consumer packaged goods, the long-term sales effects of price changes are stronger during downturns, both on own-brand sales and on cross-brand sales. For advertising, the long-term effect on own sales becomes stronger during expansions. Over time, the short-term sales response to price changes has become stronger. These effects differ across brand types (premium vs. value; mass vs. niche) and product classes (beverages, personal care, …), which offers diversification opportunities.
Contributors	Harald J. van Heerde, Massey University, Maarten J. Gijsenberg, University of Groningen, Marnik G. Dekimpe, Tilburg University and Catholic University of Leuven, and Jan-Benedict E.M. Steenkamp, University of North Carolina at Chapel Hill

Reference   van Heerde, Harald J., Maarten J. Gijsenberg, Marnik G. Dekimpe, and Jan-Benedict E.M. Steenkamp (2013), "Advertising and Price Effectiveness over the Business Cycle." *Journal of Marketing Research* 50 (2), 177–93

3

Customer Satisfaction and Product Reviews

Customer Satisfaction and Business Performance

Customer satisfaction with firms, as obtained by the American Customer Satisfaction Index, is a significant predictor (explaining 5–9% of the variance) of these firms' future accounting cash flow levels and variability, sales growth, and gross margins, as well as their financial market Tobin's Q (firm's market value to the replacement cost of its assets) and total shareholder returns.

Evidence base	A number of different analyses of over 200 firms in the American Customer Satisfaction Index from 1994 to 2003
Managerial implications	Achieving high levels of customer satisfaction has significant financial pay-offs in terms of accounting-based measures of financial performance and financial-market-based measures of shareholder value.
Contributors	Neil A. Morgan, Indiana University, and Lopo Rego, University of Iowa
References	Gruca, Thomas S., and Lopo L. Rego (2005), "Customer Satisfaction, Cash Flow, and Shareholder Value." *Journal of Marketing* 69 (3), 115–30
	Morgan, Neil A., and Lopo L. Rego (2006), "The Value of Different Customer Satisfaction and Loyalty Metrics in Predicting Business Performance." *Marketing Science* 25 (5), 426–39

Customer Satisfaction and Market Share

The average correlation between customer satisfaction and market share is −.18. It is higher for product-focused firms and lower for service-focused firms and those selling less frequently purchased products and services.

Evidence base	Analysis of 200+ firms in the American Customer Satisfaction Index from 1994 to 2003
Managerial implications	The positive impact of raising customer satisfaction on demand is usually outweighed by the difficulty of meeting the greater preference heterogeneity of a wider customer base. Using differentiated offerings for different segments in the customer base or mass customization approaches may enable firms to overcome these difficulties.
Contributors	Neil A. Morgan, Indiana University, Lopo Rego, University of Iowa, and Claes Fornell, University of Michigan
References	Fornell, Claes (1995), "The Quality of Economic Output: Empirical Generalizations about Its Distribution and Relationship to Market Share." *Marketing Science* 14 (3), 203–11 Rego, Lopo L., Neil A. Morgan, and Claes Fornell (2013), "Reexamining the Market Share–Customer Satisfaction Relationship." *Journal of Marketing* 77 (5), 1–20

Service Failure and Customer Compensation

Compensation for a service failure (a substandard service performance as a result of either the service provider or an external factor) enhances repurchase intentions only when the company is responsible for the failure and the failure occurs frequently (weighted $\eta = .36$). If the failure occurs infrequently or the company is not responsible, compensation does not affect repurchase intentions.

Evidence base	Meta-analysis of four studies. Additionally, file drawer statistics indicate that it would require 45 null studies to reduce the significance level to .05 level.
Managerial implications	Companies must maintain well-developed service recovery strategies (i.e., compensation, apology) to manage consumers' post-failure evaluations, but they also need to know exactly when to use them. When the failure is an infrequent occurrence or the company is not responsible for it, consumers do not expect to be compensated. Thus, compensation may have minimum to no impact and be a wasted resource.
Contributors	Dhruv Grewal, Babson College, Anne Roggeveen, Babson College, and Michael Tsiros, University of Miami and ALBA Graduate Business School
Reference	Grewal, Dhruv, Anne L. Roggeveen, and Michael Tsiros (2008), "The Effect of Compensation on Repurchase Intentions in Service Recovery." *Journal of Retailing* 84 (4), 424–34

Buyer–Supplier Relationships

Effect size refers to the strength of the relationship between two factors or variables. Satisfaction with buyer–supplier business-to-business (B-to-B) relationships is enhanced by trust (effect size = .64), commitment (effect size = .41), and dependence (effect size = .34). Conflict in buyer–supplier B-to-B relationships is directly reduced by trust (effect size = –.69) and commitment (effect size = –.57). Trust in buyer–supplier B-to-B relationships is enhanced by cooperation (effect size = .55) and dedicated investments made for the particular relationships that have limited value outside the relationship, i.e., transaction-specific investments (effect size = .26). Commitment in buyer–supplier B-to-B relationships is enhanced by trust (effect size = .59), dependence (effect size = .31), and transaction-specific investments (effect size = .35), and reduced by environmental uncertainty (effect size = –.16).

Evidence base	Meta-analysis of 114 measurement error corrected and sample size weighted correlations from 102 studies consisting of 26,828 B-to-B relationships
Managerial implications	Satisfaction and continuity intentions in buyer–supplier B-to-B relationships are driven primarily by relational factors. Environmental factors play a very minor role.
Contributors	Kapil Tuli, Singapore Management University, and Sundar Bharadwaj, University of Georgia
Reference	Tuli, Kapil, and Sundar Bharadwaj (2007), "Theory and Methodological Artifacts in Customer-Firm Relationships: A Meta-Analytical Review and Integrative Extension." Atlanta, Ga.: Emory University, Goizueta Business School, Working Paper

Relationship Marketing

The average correlation coefficient (sample-weighted reliability adjusted) between the strength of a customer's relationship with a seller (i.e., trust and commitment) and (1) customer loyalty is .52, and (2) objective business performance is .35.

Evidence base	Meta-analysis of approximately 20,000 seller–customer relationships
Managerial implications	The strength of the seller–customer relationship has a strong impact on customer loyalty and performance.
Contributor	Robert W. Palmatier, University of Washington
Reference	Palmatier, Robert W., Rajiv P. Dant, Dhruv Grewal, and Kenneth R. Evans (2006), "Factors Influencing the Effectiveness of Relationship Marketing: A Meta-Analysis." *Journal of Marketing* 70 (4), 136–53

Online Trust

Consumer trust in online firms mediates the effects of site design on behavioral intent (intent to try or repeat purchase). Navigation/presentation, advice, and brand are as important as privacy and security in establishing trust, but importance varies by product category. Navigation is more important on information-intensive sites (e.g., sports, portals). Brand is more important in high-involvement categories (e.g., autos and finance) and privacy is most important on information-risk sites (e.g., travel).

Evidence base	25 sites across eight categories and 6,831 consumer interviews
Managerial implications	Consumer trust in an Internet site is important to achieving sales. Trust is dependent not only on privacy and security, but also on good navigation, impartial advice, and brand strength. Relative importance depends on site category. Site design should receive careful design and testing efforts.
Contributor	Glen L. Urban, MIT
Reference	Yakov, Bart, Venkatesh Shankar, Fareena Sultan, and Glen L. Urban (2005), "Are the Drivers and Role of Online Trust the Same for All Web Sites and Consumers? A Large-Scale Exploratory Empirical Study." *Journal of Marketing* 69 (4), 133–52

Product Reviews and Sales Elasticities

Sales elasticities calculated on review valence (E_s = .69) are significantly higher than those calculated on review volume (E_s = .35). When factors such as website and involvement are considered, products on third-party websites and high involvement products produce significantly higher sales elasticities.

Evidence base	A meta-analysis of 26 empirical studies, yielding 443 sales elasticities
Managerial implications	Retailers must deliver a quality product that meets or exceeds brand promises. Additionally, mechanisms must be in place to detect service or product failures because dissatisfied customers are likely to vent, leading potential customers to go elsewhere to satisfy their needs. Finally, since potential customers may interpret a greater number of positive reviews as an accurate assessment of the service or product, retailers should encourage customers with a favorable experience to post a review.
Contributors	Kristopher Floyd, University of Texas at Arlington, Ryan Freling, University of Texas at Dallas, and Traci Freling, University of Texas at Arlington
Reference	Floyd, Kristopher, Ryan Freling, Saad Alhoqail, Hyun Young Cho, and Traci Freling (2014), "How Online Product Reviews Affect Retail Sales: A Meta-analysis." *Journal of Retailing* 90 (2), 217–32

Electronic Word-of-Mouth Elasticity

Electronic word-of-mouth (from sources such as blogs, forums, social networking sites, and online product reviews) volume elasticity averages .236 and valence elasticity averages .417. The volume and valence elasticities are higher for privately consumed (volume = 1.036, valence = 1.205), low-trialability products (volume = .618, valence = 1.235) that operate in less competitive industries (volume = .71, valence = .733) and whose reviews are carried on independent review sites (volume = .91, valence = .602). Furthermore, volume elasticities are higher for durable goods (volume = 1.32) and for reviews on specialized review sites (volume = 2.94), whereas valence elasticities are greater for community-based sites (valence = 1.4).

Evidence base	A meta-analysis of 51 studies involving 339 volume and 271 valence elasticities
Managerial implications	1. Managers of durable, low-trialability, privately consumed products can benefit more from electronic word-of-mouth (eWOM), so they should actively monitor social media metrics.
	2. Managers in industries in which competitive pressures are intense should be wary of relying on eWOM alone for generating sales and rely more on traditional means of advertising and promotion.
	3. The type of platform that carries the information affects eWOM elasticities, which demonstrates that not all social media and eWOM are created equal. Managers should carefully consider the type of social media platforms to deliver brand and product information.

4. Ignoring consumer complaints on the Internet can be a risky proposition. This not only explains the growing roles of "social media managers" or "online community managers" in organizations, but also prompts laggard firms to pay special attention to this aspect of firm-related consumer-to-consumer communications.

Contributors	Ya You, College of Charleston, Gautham G. Vadakkepatt, George Mason University, and Amit M. Joshi, University of Central Florida
Reference	You, Ya, Gautham G. Vadakkepatt, and Amit M. Joshi (2015), "A Meta-Analysis of Electronic Word-of-Mouth Elasticity." *Journal of Marketing* 79 (2), 19–39

Product-Harm Crises

A product-harm crisis may cause multiple jeopardies for the affected brand: (1) a loss in baseline sales, (2) a reduced own-marketing-mix effectiveness (e.g., lower advertising impact), (3) an increased sensitivity to rival brands' marketing-mix activities, and (4) a decreased cross impact of the own-marketing-mix instruments on the sales of competing, unaffected brands.

Managers of both affected and non-affected brands often increase their advertising support or decrease their price in the wake of a product-harm crisis, in an attempt to regain lost customers, or to benefit from the misfortune of their competitors. Others increase their prices in an effort to safeguard the brands' revenues. The adequacy of any adjustment is highly context-dependent, and varies with the extent of negative publicity surrounding the event, and whether the affected brand had to publicly acknowledge blame. In addition, managers should take the altered effectiveness into account when deciding on the magnitude of the adjustment.

Evidence base	60+ fast-moving consumer good product-harm crises
Managerial implications	When deciding on post-crisis price and advertising adjustments, managers should take into account (1) that the magnitude of the relevant (own and/or cross) elasticities may have changed, (2) the objective of the marketing-mix change, i.e., brand-share or category-sales recovery, (3) the extent of negative publicity surrounding the crisis, and (4) whether or not blame had to be acknowledged.

In particular, in a low-publicity product-harm case, where blame had to be admitted, brands and categories are not advised to increase advertising, as the instrument becomes considerably less effective. However, in the opposite case (high publicity, no blame) an advertising increase is recommended. As for price, brand price decreases are only recommended when blame had to be acknowledged, whereas category price decreases are recommended in all cases, and even more so in case of high publicity.

Contributors	Marnik G. Dekimpe, Tilburg University and Catholic University of Leuven, and Harald J. van Heerde, Massey University
References	Cleeren, Kathleen, Marnik G. Dekimpe, and Kristiaan Helsen (2008), "Weathering Product-Harm Crises." *Journal of the Academy of Marketing Science* 36 (2), 262–70
	Cleeren, Kathleen, Harald J. van Heerde, and Marnik G. Dekimpe (2013), "Rising from the Ashes: How Brands and Categories Can Overcome Product-Harm Crises." *Journal of Marketing* 77 (2), 58–77
	van Heerde, Harald, J., Kristiaan Helsen, and Marnik G. Dekimpe (2007), "The Impact of a Product-Harm Crisis on Marketing Effectiveness." *Marketing Science* 26 (2), 230–45

4

Objective and Perceived Quality

Customers' Objective and Subjective Knowledge

The average correlation between what consumers know (objective knowledge) and what they think they know (subjective/perceived knowledge) about various products, services, and other marketing contexts is .37.

Evidence base	Meta-analysis of 51 prior studies
Managerial implications	Consumers' beliefs regarding their level of knowledge of various products, services, and other marketing contexts are related to the amount of their actual knowledge, but not strongly. Combining the meta-analysis results with Ailawadi, Dant, and Grewal's (2004) research, self-report data are likely to demonstrate modest correspondence with objective data. For example, a firm's self-reported innovation capability is probably positively but only modestly related to its actual innovation capability.
Contributors	William O. Bearden, University of South Carolina, Jay P. Carlson, Union Graduate College, David M. Hardesty, University of Kentucky, and Leslie H. Vincent, Eastern Kentucky University
References	Ailawadi, Kusum L., Rajiv P. Dant, and Dhruv Grewal (2004), "The Difference Between Perceptual and Objective Performance Measures: An Empirical Analysis." Cambridge, Mass.: Marketing Science Institute, Report No. 04–103

Carlson, Jay P., Leslie H. Vincent, David M. Hardesty, and William O. Bearden (2009), "Objective and Subjective Knowledge Relationships: A Quantitative Analysis of Consumer Research Findings." *Journal of Consumer Research* 35 (5), 864–76

Objective and Perceived Quality

A change in objective quality is not fully reflected in customer perceptions of quality until after about six years on average. Across categories, the range is three to nine years. In the first year, only about 20% of the total effect is realized. These effects are larger and occur more quickly for decreases in quality relative to increases in quality. High-reputation brands are rewarded three years faster for quality increases and punished one year more slowly for quality decreases relative to lower-reputation brands.

Evidence base	241 products in 46 product categories over 12 years
Managerial implications	A firm's investments in product quality will pay off over the long term. High-reputation brands enjoy an advantage when competing on quality because consumers update their favorable perceptions more quickly. Firms should track both objective quality and perceived quality, along with its associated lags, in order to develop the appropriate quality strategy.
Contributors	Debanjan Mitra, University of Florida, and Peter N. Golder, Dartmouth College
Reference	Mitra, Debanjan, and Peter N. Golder (2006), "How Does Objective Quality Affect Perceived Quality? Short-Term Effects, Long-Term Effects, and Asymmetries." *Marketing Science* 25 (3), 230–47

Impact of Product Quality on Price

The correlation between price and quality varies substantially across products (categories) and can be negative for some products. It generally increases with the level of information in the market. It is higher for durables, products with a high price range, and products that can be inspected outside their package.

Evidence base	A meta-analysis of nine studies, covering 1,365 products, over a 41-year period, from 1939 to 1980
Managerial implications	Because of the difficulty of search, prices are not always congruent with the underlying quality of the products. Public policy makers should consider increasing the availability of information on product quality. Managers may be able to charge higher prices for products of inferior quality in product markets where quality is difficult to ascertain or costs of search for quality remain high.
Contributor	Gerard J. Tellis, University of Southern California
Reference	Tellis, Gerard J., and Birger Wernerfelt (1987), "Competitive Price and Quality under Asymmetric Information." *Marketing Science* (6) 3, 240–53

Impact of Product Quality on Market Share

Markets are reasonably efficient in terms of market share response to product quality, even in the presence of network effects. In particular, market share leadership changes often, switches in market share leadership closely follow switches in quality leadership, and the best quality brands, not the ones to enter first, dominate their markets. Network effects enhance the positive effect of quality.

Evidence base	An analysis of 19 categories, in personal computer product and services markets, from 1982 to 1999
Managerial implications	The effects of path dependence or network effects may be exaggerated. Managers need to be cognizant of the quality of their products in markets, even in the presence of network effects or path dependence. Market leadership can change easily and quickly with the entry of new products with superior quality or improvements in quality of established products.
Contributor	Gerard J. Tellis, University of Southern California
Reference	Tellis, Gerard J., Yiding Yin, and Rakesh Niraj (2009), "Does Quality Win: Network Effects versus Quality in High Tech Markets." *Journal of Marketing Research* 46 (2), 135–49

5

Market Share

Performance Evolution

Sales levels tend to evolve over multiple years (68% of cases); this is especially true for category or industry sales (92% of cases). However, market share tends to be stable over time (78% of cases).

Evidence base	Meta-analysis of over 400 prior analyses
Managerial implications	Long-term sales growth for a brand is derived mainly from category growth. While temporary share gains and losses are common, it is difficult to generate sustained long-term market-share growth in mature markets.
Contributors	Marnik G. Dekimpe, Tilburg University and Catholic University of Leuven, and Dominique M. Hanssens, UCLA
Reference	Dekimpe, Marnik G., and Dominique M. Hanssens (1995), "Empirical Generalizations About Market Evolution and Stationarity." *Marketing Science* 14 (3) (Part 2 of 2), G109–21

Market Share and Profitability

Profitability is not a direct function of market share. While the average weighted market share–profit elasticity is .35, when factors such as intangibles (e.g., brands, customer relationships, intellectual property, etc.) are also modeled, the elasticity is reduced to zero.

Evidence base	Meta-analysis of 276 prior studies
Managerial implications	Profit and market share are each simultaneously positively driven by intangibles, goods/service quality, product line breadth, sales force expenditures, and the growth of the market. Thus, improvements in any of these areas can expand both share and profitability. Attempts at increasing market share alone may not yield greater profitability.
Contributors	David Szymanski, University of Cincinnati, Sundar Bharadwaj, University of Georgia, and P. Rajan Varadarajan, Texas A&M University
Reference	Szymanski, David M., Sundar G. Bharadwaj, and P. Rajan Varadarajan (1993), "An Analysis of the Market Share–Profitability Relationship." *Journal of Marketing* 57 (3), 1–18

Market Leadership

Of the leading brands in 1923, more failed than remained market leaders by 1997. Of the top three brands in 1923, more failed than remained among the top five brands in 1997. Market-share ranks over this prolonged period are not stable. Non-durable goods have higher leadership persistence and a lower failure rate than durable goods. Brand leaders in food and beverages perform above average and brand leaders in clothing perform below average.

Evidence base	650 brands in 100 categories over seven decades
Managerial implications	Over extended periods, leading brands face a meaningful risk of losing their market leadership. Therefore, companies with leading brands must continue to monitor and invest in them. Companies without leading brands should continuously evaluate selective brand investments aimed at supplanting current leaders.
Contributor	Peter N. Golder, Dartmouth College
Reference	Golder, Peter N. (2000), "Historical Method in Marketing Research with New Evidence on Long-Term Market Share Stability." *Journal of Marketing Research* 37 (2), 156–72

Brand Geography: Persistence

For consumer packaged goods, the historic order-of-entry of the current largest surviving brands predicts the rank-order of their current shares in a geographic market. On average, a mature (90 years) CPG brand's share in its most geographically remote market is roughly 20 points lower than its share in its city of origin. Brand shares correlate with advertising across markets, but not with promotional variables.

Likely explanations of such persistence include early mover advantage (most CPG brands studied were launched in the late 19th or early 20th centuries), subsequent pre-emptive marketing (advertising) and/or distribution investments and enduring consumer brand-buying habits.

Evidence base	Monthly scanner data from AC Nielsen (Scantrack level and account level) and IRI (BehaviorScan Level); historic data on brand roll-out from company archives, published business histories, public archives and the Internet; brand quality measures from Young & Rubicam
Managerial implications	This persistence in geographic market share variation is consistent with product innovation and advertising having a greater long-term impact on market share than do pricing and trade promotions. After a major innovation, the entry "clock" can be reset. In the absence of such innovation, however, order of entry may largely determine subsequent market share.
Contributors	Bart J. Bronnenberg, Tilburg University, and Jean-Pierre H. Dubé, University of Chicago

References

Bronnenberg, Bart J., Sanjay Dhar, and Jean-Pierre Dubé (2007), "Consumer Packaged Goods in the United States: National Brands, Local Branding." *Journal of Marketing Research* 44 (1), 4–13

Bronnenberg, Bart J., Sanjay K. Dhar, and Jean-Pierre Dubé (2009), "Brand History, Geography, and the Persistence of CPG Brand Shares." *Journal of Political Economy* 117 (1), 87–115

Bronnenberg, Bart J., Sanjay K. Dhar, and Jean-Pierre Dubé (2011), "Endogenous Sunk Costs and the Geographic Differences in the Market Structures of CPG Categories," *Quantitative Marketing and Economics* 9 (1), 1–23

Brand Geography: Consumer Loyalty

For brands of consumer packaged goods (CPG), market share dominance varies greatly across U.S. geographic regions. Also, market share dominance can persist across many decades, even in the presence of physically similar products differentiated by little more than the brand name itself.

One potential mechanism for this persistence in dominance is the persistence in consumer brand preferences specifically. The high level of migration in the U.S. can be exploited to test for consumer taste persistence. Consumers moving from one region to another tend to retain the brand preferences of their region of origin. This retained component decays extremely slowly: the half-life of having lived in a specific region for a year is 27 years.

Evidence base	45,000 households in the AC Nielsen Homescan panel, 240 product categories
Managerial implications	A large part of the persistence in geographic market share variation is due to consumer preferences. Consumer preferences form an important component of brand capital. Consumer preferences are sticky enough to sustain brand shares even in the presence of large supply side shocks. Firms launching new products should invest in getting consumers to buy and use their products to build early brand capital.
Contributors	Bart J. Bronnenberg, Tilburg University, and Jean-Pierre H. Dubé, University of Chicago
References	Bronnenberg, Bart J., Sanjay K. Dhar, and Jean-Pierre Dubé (2009), "Brand History, Geography, and the Persistence of CPG Brand Shares." *Journal of Political Economy* 117 (1), 87–115

Bronnenberg, Bart J., Jean-Pierre Dubé, and Matthew Gentzkow (2012), "The Evolution of Brand Preferences: Evidence from Consumer Migration." *American Economic Review* 102 (6), 2472–508

Brand Geography: Concentration

Even in the largest geographic markets the largest firm typically has at least 20% of the share of volume sold. Within a category, one or two advertising-supported brands typically dominate each geographic market regardless of market size. Within a category, eight or nine non-advertising brands typically operate in a geographic market, with the number escalating as market size increases.

Evidence base	Monthly data for 31 CPG product categories across the 50 largest Nielsen Scantracks from 1993 to 1996
Managerial implications	Competition is driven more by the intensity of marketing efforts (e.g., advertising) by a few large firms than by the sheer number of firms competing in a given category and geographic market. While larger, dominant firms must compete with heavier marketing investments, smaller brands can still survive without such investments by catering to consumers who are unwilling to pay a premium for branded goods.
Contributors	Bart J. Bronnenberg, Tilburg University, and Jean-Pierre H. Dubé, University of Chicago
References	Bronnenberg, Bart J., Sanjay Dhar, and Jean-Pierre Dubé (2007), "Consumer Packaged Goods in the United States: National Brands, Local Branding." *Journal of Marketing Research* 44 (1), 4–13
	Bronnenberg, Bart J., Sanjay K. Dhar, and Jean-Pierre Dubé (2009), "Brand History, Geography, and the Persistence of CPG Brand Shares." *Journal of Political Economy* 117 (1), 87–115

Bronnenberg, Bart J., Sanjay K. Dhar, and Jean-Pierre Dubé (2011), "Endogenous Sunk Costs and the Geographic Differences in the Market Structures of CPG Categories," *Quantitative Marketing and Economics* 9 (1), 1–23

6

Order of Entry

Pioneer Survival Rates

For industrial goods businesses, market pioneers tend to have higher survival rates than later entrants. This result is not supported when pioneering a really new product-market, which accounts for 25% of innovations.

Evidence base	264 new industrial product-markets from the *Thomas Register of American Manufacturers*
Managerial implications	While first-mover advantages help a market pioneer survive, these advantages are offset by the market and technological uncertainties associated with pioneering a really new market. For market pioneers, the overall risk-and-return profile is more encouraging for incremental innovation markets. This is because incrementally new products are typically developed in response to an already existing felt need and they tend to be based on a refinement or extension of existing technology. Hence, pioneers in incremental innovation markets have relatively low risk and higher pioneer survival rates.
Contributors	Manohar U. Kalwani, Purdue University, and William T. Robinson, Purdue University
References	Min, Sungwook, Manohar U. Kalwani, and William T. Robinson (2006), "Market Pioneer and Early Follower Survival Risks: A Contingency Analysis of Really New Versus Incrementally New Product-Markets." *Journal of Marketing* 70 (1), 15–33

Robinson, William T., and Sungwook Min (2002), "Is the First to Market the First to Fail? Empirical Evidence for Industrial Goods Businesses." *Journal of Marketing Research* 39 (1), 120–8

Pioneering in Business-to-Business Markets

For manufacturing businesses that survive, market pioneers tend to have higher market shares than later entrants.

Evidence base	Major markets in North America, the Asia Pacific region, and Europe. The North American results are based on nine research studies; the other results are based on 2,419 firms in nine countries.
Managerial implications	For market pioneers that survive, their innovation efforts are often rewarded with a higher market share. Pioneer product line breadth advantages are more sustainable than either product quality advantages or patent protection. Thus, when a market pioneer develops a broad product line early, it can force later entrants to serve narrow market niches.
Contributors	Manohar U. Kalwani, Purdue University, and William T. Robinson, Purdue University
References	Kalyanaram, Gurumurthy, William T. Robinson, and Glen L. Urban (1995), "Order of Market Entry: Established Empirical Generalizations, Emerging Empirical Generalizations, and Future Research." *Marketing Science* 14 (3) (Part 2 of 2), G212–21
	Song, X. Michael, C. Anthony Di Benedetto, and Yuzhen Lisa Zhao (1999), "Pioneering Advantages in Manufacturing and Service Industries: Empirical Evidence from Nine Countries." *Strategic Management Journal* 20 (9), 811–35

Order of Entry and Market Share

On average, a pioneer has a 4.2% point advantage in market share over a later entrant. This effect is larger for strategic business units than for brands. The effect size is inflated when product line breadth and marketing expenditures are not included in the model. The effect size is lower when entry is measured in actual sequence, and not aggregated pioneer/non-pioneer.

Evidence base	Meta-analysis of 23 studies providing 64 elasticities from prior analyses
Managerial implications	Entering markets as a pioneer pays off in terms of market share advantage, especially for strategic business units. Pioneering advantages are augmented by service quality, vertical integration, R&D expenditures, shared facilities and customers, market growth, and frequently purchased products.
Contributors	David Szymanski, University of Cincinnati, Lisa Troy, Texas A&M University, and Sundar Bharadwaj, University of Georgia
Reference	Szymanski, David M., Lisa C. Troy, and Sundar G. Bharadwaj (1995), "Order of Entry and Business Performance: An Empirical Synthesis and Reexamination." *Journal of Marketing* 59 (4), 17–33

Order of Entry: Consumer Packaged Goods and Pharmaceuticals

For consumer packaged goods and prescription anti-ulcer drugs, the entrant's forecasted market share divided by the first entrant's market share roughly equals 1 divided by the square root of the order of market entry.

Evidence base	129 consumer brands and 189 monthly observations from the anti-ulcer market (8 brands)
Managerial implications	In these markets, specific share-decline penalties for late entry can be estimated by the 1 over the square root of N rule (where N is the order of entry, N = 2, 3, …). These penalties can be reduced by increased advertising and sales expenditures and better product performance and positioning.
Contributor	Glen L. Urban, MIT
References	Kalyanaram, Gurumurthy, and Glen Urban (1992), "Dynamic Effects of the Order of Entry on Market Share, Trial Penetration, and Repeat Purchases for Frequently Purchased Consumer Goods." *Marketing Science* 11 (3), 235–50
	Urban, Glen, Ernst R. Berndt, Linda T. Bui, and David H. Reiley (1997), "The Roles of Marketing, Product Quality and Price Competition in the Growth and Composition of the U.S. Anti-Ulcer Drug Industry." In *The Economics of New Goods*, eds. Timothy Bresnahan and Robert J. Gordan. Chicago, Ill.: University of Chicago Press for the National Bureau of Economic Research
	Urban, Glen L., Theresa Carter, Steven Gaskin, and Zofia Mucha (1986), "Market Share Rewards to Pioneering Brands: An Empirical Analysis and Strategic Implications." *Management Science* 32 (6), 645–59

Order of Entry: Mature Consumer and Industrial Goods

For mature consumer and industrial goods, there is a negative relationship between order of market entry and market share.

Evidence base	Analysis of 129 consumer brands over 36 categories and PIMS data for 1,209 industrial and 371 consumer businesses
Managerial implications	Later entrants should expect a lower share if they introduce similar products to successful pioneers. These penalties can be reduced by increased advertising and sales expenditures and better product performance and positioning.
Contributor	Glen L. Urban, MIT
References	Kalyanaram, Gurumurthy, and Glen Urban (1992), "Dynamic Effects of the Order of Entry on Market Share, Trial Penetration, and Repeat Purchases for Frequently Purchased Consumer Goods." *Marketing Science* 11 (3), 235–50
	Robinson, William T. (1988), "Sources of Market Pioneer Advantages: The Case of Industrial Goods Industries." *Journal of Marketing Research* 25 (1), 87–94
	Robinson, William T., and Claes Fornell (1985), "Sources of Market Pioneer Advantages in Consumer Goods Industries." *Journal of Marketing Research* 22 (3), 305–17
	Urban, Glen L., Theresa Carter, Steven Gaskin, and Zofia Mucha (1986), "Market Share Rewards to Pioneering Brands: An Empirical Analysis and Strategic Implications." *Management Science* 32 (6), 645–59

Order-of-Entry Effects

The impact of order of entry on long-term market performance is mixed. An initial entrant has a significant market share advantage, with subsequent entrants' share about 1 divided by the square root of the order of entry. This effect declines over time and it is not as strong (although it remains significant) if (1) the reasons that explain these effects are included in the analysis, i.e., considering entry time as endogenous and (2) one accounts for survival bias. However, these effects are explained almost entirely by asymmetries in marketing mix effectiveness. There is no evidence of order-of-entry effect on the long-term survival rate. Pioneers have a short-term profit advantage but a disadvantage in the long term (the production and SG&A cost disadvantage overcome the purchasing advantages).

Evidence base	PIMS data (Robinson and Fornell 1985; Moore, Boulding, and Goodstein 1991; Boulding and Christen 2003); 5 durable and non-durable categories (Urban et al. 1986; Bowman and Gatignon 1996); 50 durable and non-durable categories (Golder and Tellis 1993)
Managerial implications	There is a significant advantage in terms of market share for entering markets early but subsequent entrants can overcome their disadvantage through innovation and marketing. The pioneer must be ready to accept higher costs in the long term.
Contributors	Hubert Gatignon, INSEAD, and Douglas Bowman, Emory University

References

Main effect of pioneering or order of entry:

Kalyanaram, Gurumurthy, William T. Robinson, and Glen L. Urban (1995), "Order of Market Entry: Established Empirical Generalizations, Emerging Empirical Generalizations, and Future Research." *Marketing Science* 14 (3) (Part 2 of 2), G212–21

Robinson, William T., and Claes Fornell (1985), "Sources of Market Pioneer Advantages in Consumer Goods Industries." *Journal of Marketing Research* 22 (3), 305–17

Urban, Glen L., Theresa Carter, Steven Gaskin, and Zofia Mucha (1986), "Market Share Rewards to Pioneering Brands: An Empirical Analysis and Strategic Implications." *Management Science* 32 (6), 645–59

Market entry time is not exogenous:

Boulding, William, and Markus Christen (2003), "Sustainable Pioneering Advantage? Profit Implications of Market Entry Order." *Marketing Science* 22 (3), 371–92

Moore, Michael J., William Boulding, and Ronald C. Goodstein (1991), "Pioneering and Market Share: Is Entry Time Endogenous and Does It Matter?" *Journal of Marketing Research* 28 (1), 97–104

Accounting for survivor bias:

Golder, Peter N., and Gerard J. Tellis (1993), "Pioneer Advantage: Marketing Logic or Marketing Legend?" *Journal of Marketing Research* 30 (2), 158–70

Vander Werf, Pieter A., and John F. Mahon (1997), "Meta-Analysis of the Impact of Research Methods on Findings of First-Mover Advantage." *Management Science* 43 (11), 1510–9

Main effect of entry time is largely as a moderator of marketing mix effectiveness:

Bowman, Douglas, and Hubert Gatignon (1996), "Order of Entry as a Moderator of the Effect of the Marketing Mix on Market Share." *Marketing Science* 15 (3), 222–42

First-mover Advantage

In really new product categories, market pioneers' failure rate is 64%, with an average long-run market share of 6% and leadership incidence of 9%. Instead of first-mover advantage, the superior performance of enduring market leaders is driven by five other factors: vision of the mass market, managerial persistence, relentless innovation, financial commitment, and asset leverage.

Evidence base	66 product categories: 24 digital, high technology, 41 business-to-consumer, 25 combined business-to-business and business-to-consumer
Managerial implications	Companies should not rely on possible first-mover advantages for their success. Instead, first movers and later entrants should focus on identifying a mass market, continuous innovation, and persistent application of resources to achieve and sustain market leadership.
Contributors	Peter N. Golder, Dartmouth College, and Gerard J. Tellis, University of Southern California
References	Golder, Peter N., and Gerard J. Tellis (1993), "Pioneer Advantage: Marketing Logic or Marketing Legend." *Journal of Marketing Research* 30 (2), 158–70
	Tellis, Gerard J., and Peter N. Golder (2001), *Will and Vision: How Latecomers Grow to Dominate Markets*. New York, N.Y.: McGraw Hill

7

Sales Diffusion and Social Influence

	Adoption/Diffusion Pattern of New Durables
	In the Bass diffusion model, the average coefficient of innovation (p) is .03 and the average coefficient of imitation (q) is .30. The values p and q differ by product, with q typically higher for industrial products. The value p is stable over time, while q may be increasing.
Evidence base	Meta-analysis of 213 diffusion models reported in 15 articles published in the 1970s and the 1980s. Most were consumer durables.
Managerial implications	Sales to first-time buyers will peak five to six years from the start of substantial sales.
Contributor	Donald R. Lehmann, Columbia University
Reference	Sultan, Fareena, John U. Farley, and Donald R. Lehmann (1990), "A Meta-Analysis of Applications of Diffusion Models." *Journal of Marketing Research* 27 (1), 70–7

Global Diffusion

The reported mean value of the coefficient of innovation (p), from meta-analysis studies, is .03. It is higher for developed than developing countries and for European countries than for the U.S. The reported mean value of the coefficient of imitation (q), from meta-analysis studies, is .40. It is higher for developing countries than developed countries and for industrial/medical innovations than for durables and other products.

Evidence base	Several published reports on meta-analyses of estimates of the Bass diffusion model
Managerial implications	The diffusion process is affected by word-of-mouth to a larger extent than by innate innovativeness of consumers. Diffusion speed is faster in developed countries than developing countries. It may be best to launch new products earlier in developed countries than in developing countries.
Contributors	Deepa Chandrasekaran, University of Texas at San Antonio, and Gerard J. Tellis, University of Southern California
References	Chandrasekaran, Deepa, and Tellis, Gerard J. (2007), "A Critical Review of Marketing Research on Diffusion of New Products." In *Review of Marketing Research*, ed. Naresh Malhotra, vol. 3, 39–81. Armonk, N.Y.: M.E. Sharpe Inc.
	Sultan, Fareena, John U. Farley, and Donald Lehmann (1990), "A Meta-Analysis of Applications of Diffusion Models." *Journal of Marketing Research* 27 (1), 70–7
	Talukdar, Debabrata, K. Sudhir, and Andrew Ainslie (2002), "Investigating New Product Diffusion Across Products and Countries." *Marketing Science* 21 (1), 97–114

Van den Bulte, Christophe, and Stefan Stremersch (2004), "Social Contagion and Income Heterogeneity in New Product Diffusion: A Meta-Analytic Test." *Marketing Science* 23 (4), 530–44

International Diffusion

The average penetration potential for developing countries is about one-third (.17 versus .52) of that for developed countries. It takes developing countries on average 17.9% more time to achieve peak sales (19.25 years versus 16.3 years). Thus, despite the well-known positive effect of product introduction delays on diffusion speed, developing countries still experience a slower adoption rate, compared to that of developed countries. Several macro-environmental variables influence penetration potential and speed. For example, a 1% change in international trade changes the penetration potential by about .5%. A similar growth in urbanization level changes the penetration potential by .2%.

Evidence base	Data on six new product launches (VCR, CD, microwaves, camcorders, faxes, and cellphones) in 31 countries between 1975 and 1997
Managerial implications	Managers can use this information to fine-tune their expectations about diffusion in different countries as they roll out new product launches, and to better predict the demand over multiple years.
Contributor	Andrew Ainslie, University of Rochester
Reference	Talukdar, Debabrata, Andrew Ainslie, and K. Sudhir (2002), "Investigating New Product Diffusion across Products and Countries." *Marketing Science* 21 (1), 97–114

Sales Takeoff

The early sales histories of really new consumer durables exhibit consistent regularities including a sharp sales takeoff after 12 years on average (6 years for more recent categories) and a slowdown after an additional 8 years. At takeoff, average sales increase by 428% and market penetration is 2.9%. At slowdown, sales tend to decrease by 15% and market penetration is 34%. Product categories with larger sales increases at takeoff tend to have larger sales declines at slowdown.

Evidence base	31 really new consumer durables (household appliances and consumer electronics) for takeoff and 30 similar categories for slowdown
Managerial implications	Previous sales patterns provide useful benchmarks for today's new product categories. The extended time-to-takeoff requires patience and careful planning. An unusually long time-to-takeoff may indicate that the new product should be withdrawn. Managers should expect a decrease in sales about eight years after takeoff and plan for this slowdown by adjusting manufacturing, sales force, inventory, and marketing.
Contributors	Peter N. Golder, Dartmouth College, and Gerard J. Tellis, University of Southern California
References	Golder, Peter N., and Gerard J. Tellis (1997), "Will It Ever Fly? Modeling the Takeoff of Really New Consumer Durables." *Marketing Science* 16 (3), 256–70
	Golder, Peter N., and Gerard J. Tellis (2004), "Growing, Growing, Gone: Cascades, Diffusion, and Turning Points in the Product Life Cycle." *Marketing Science* 23 (2), 207–18

Global Takeoff

The mean time-to-takeoff varies considerably between developed countries (about 7 years) and developing countries (about 12 years). Fun products (information and entertainment) take off faster than work products (home appliances). The mean time-to-takeoff for fun products is about 7 years while the mean time-to-takeoff for work products is about 12 years, across all countries. In developed countries, the mean time-to-takeoff for fun products is about 4 years, and about 8 years for work products. Within Europe, Scandinavian (Nordic) countries see the fastest takeoff, with estimates of takeoff at about 4 years for fun products and about 7 years for work products. Time-to-takeoff is converging over time, at least for developed countries.

Evidence base	16 new products (household appliances, consumer electronics, and communication services) across 31 countries plus 10 products (household appliances, consumer electronics) across 16 European countries
Managerial implications	Distinct cross-country differences in takeoff point to the need for a waterfall entry strategy (staggering the commercialization of new products across countries). It may be best to launch new products in small quick-takeoff countries, to serve as the starting point of the waterfall strategy. This approach lowers risk, provides for learning, and enables seeding of the diffusion process.
Contributors	Deepa Chandrasekaran, University of Texas at San Antonio, and Gerard J. Tellis, University of Southern California
References	Chandrasekaran, Deepa, and Gerard J. Tellis (2008), "Global Takeoff of New Products: Culture, Wealth, or Vanishing Differences? *Marketing Science* 27 (5), 844–60

Tellis, Gerard J., Stefan Stremersch, and Eden Yin (2003), "The International Takeoff of New Products: The Role of Economics, Culture, and Country Innovativeness." *Marketing Science* 22 (2), 188–208

Technological Evolution

1. Contrary to the theory of S-curves, technologies do not show evidence of a single S-shaped curve of performance improvement. Rather, they evolve through an irregular step function, with long periods of no growth in performance interspersed with performance jumps.

2. New technologies may enter above or below the performance of existing technologies. The performance curves of a pair of competing technologies rarely have a single crossing.

3. The rate of technological change and the number of new technologies increase over time.

4. New technologies come as much from new entrants as from large incumbents.

5. Each new technology introduces a sequence of random, seemingly unpredictable secondary dimensions as a new basis of competition.

Evidence base	23 technologies encompassing 1,004 technology years

Managerial implications

1. Using the S-curve to predict the performance of a technology is risky. The continuous emergence of new technologies and the steady growth of most technologies suggest that relying on the status quo is dangerous for any firm.

2. Attack from below remains a viable threat.

3. Emergence of secondary dimensions of competition is a significant threat to incumbents.

4. First-mover advantages may not be lasting because entrants introduce even more innovations than do incumbent firms.

5. Popular laws and models such as Moore's law, Kryder's law, Gompertz's law, and the logistic model are naïve generalizations of a complex phenomenon, and do not predict technology change well.

Contributors	Ashish Sood, Georgia State University, and Gerard J. Tellis, University of Southern California
References	Sood, Ashish, and Gerard J. Tellis (2005), "The S-curve of Technological Evolution: Strategic Law or Self-Fulfilling Prophecy?" Cambridge, Mass.: Marketing Science Institute, Report No. 04–116
	Sood, Ashish, and Gerard J. Tellis (2005), "Technological Evolution and Radical Innovation." *Journal of Marketing* 69 (3), 152–68
	Sood, Ashish, Gareth James, and Gerard J. Tellis (2012), "Predicting the Path of Technological Innovation: SAW Versus Moore, Bass, Gompertz, and Kryder." *Marketing Science* 31 (6), 964–79

Radical Innovations

Radical innovations take about 50 years, on average, to go from initial concept to broad-market sales. For more recent products, this duration is still 22 years. During this period, different firms tend to lead product and market development for each innovation. For example, 76% of firms that were first to commercialize an innovation were not first to commercialize it to a broader market.

Evidence base	29 radical innovations tracked from initial concept to broad market commercialization (i.e., annual sales of at least 10,000 units). Innovations were commercialized between 1838 and 1983.
Managerial implications	Early-stage investments in radical innovations are not likely to have short-run payoffs. Companies should look externally at existing concepts and prototypes for opportunities to commercialize future radical innovations.
Contributors	Peter N. Golder, Dartmouth College, Rachel Shacham, New York University, and Debanjan Mitra, University of Florida
Reference	Golder, Peter N., Rachel Shacham, and Debanjan Mitra (2009), "Innovations' Origins: When, by Whom, and How Are Radical Innovations Developed?" *Marketing Science* 28 (1), 166–79

Cross-country Differences in the Shape of the New Product Diffusion Curve

A country's culture and income distribution are related to the extent to which new products diffuse in that country according to a pronounced S-curve, measured as a higher q/p shape parameter of the Bass diffusion curve. Specifically, using the Hofstede scale for cultural orientation and the Gini coefficient for income inequality:

- For products without competing standards, higher individualism and higher uncertainty avoidance lower the q/p ratio. Higher power distance and higher masculinity increase the q/p ratio. For products with competing standards, culture does not affect the q/p ratio.

- Higher income inequality increases the q/p ratio when there are no competing standards, but lowers the q/p ratio in the presence of competing standards.

Evidence base	Meta-analysis of 293 diffusion trajectories pertaining to 52 consumer durables in 28 countries reported in 46 publications
Managerial implications	A pronounced diffusion curve (slow initial adoption followed by rapid growth) can be predicted from a country's cultural orientation and income inequality. However, the effects depend on whether the product category has competing standards or not (e.g., Betamax vs. VHS in VCRs).
Contributor	Christophe Van den Bulte, University of Pennsylvania
Reference	Van den Bulte, Christophe, and Stefan Stremersch (2004), "Social Contagion and Income Heterogeneity in New Product Diffusion: A Meta-Analytic Test." *Marketing Science* 23 (4), 530–44

Competing Standards and the Shape of the New Product Diffusion Curve

Product categories exhibiting competing standards tend to have diffusion trajectories with a more pronounced S-shape. Specifically, the presence of competing standards tends to increase the q/p shape parameter of the Bass diffusion curve by a factor of 2 to 3 and the logistic growth parameter by a factor of 2 to 2.5.

Evidence base	Meta-analysis of 293 diffusion trajectories pertaining to 52 consumer durables in 28 countries reported in 46 publications, and analysis of 31 consumer durables in the U.S.
Managerial implications	The presence of competing standards dramatically slows down early sales growth, but this is compensated by faster growth subsequently.
Contributor	Christophe Van den Bulte, University of Pennsylvania
References	Van den Bulte, Christophe (2000), "New Product Diffusion Acceleration: Measurement and Analysis." *Marketing Science* 19 (4), 366–80
	Van den Bulte, Christophe, and Stefan Stremersch (2004), "Social Contagion and Income Heterogeneity in New Product Diffusion: A Meta-Analytic Test." *Marketing Science* 23 (4), 530–44

Cross-time Differences in the Shape of the New Product Diffusion Curve

Over the last 50 years, diffusion trajectories have tended to become less S-shaped, as reflected in the q/p shape parameter of Bass diffusion curves trending downward. Specifically, for every 1-year increment in the launch time of a new product, the q/p shape parameter tends to decrease by .1%.

Evidence base	Meta-analysis of 293 diffusion trajectories pertaining to 52 consumer durables in 28 countries reported in 46 publications
Managerial implications	The extent to which new product sales growth is slow at first and accelerates only later has decreased over time and is likely to continue doing so.
Contributor	Christophe Van den Bulte, University of Pennsylvania
Reference	Van den Bulte, Christophe, and Stefan Stremersch (2004), "Social Contagion and Income Heterogeneity in New Product Diffusion: A Meta-Analytic Test." *Marketing Science* 23 (4), 530–44

Cross-time Differences in the Speed of New Product Diffusion

Over the last 50 years, the speed of diffusion has increased by about 2–3% a year. Demographic changes and increasing disposable income per household can explain much of this increase.

Evidence base	Analysis of 31 consumer durables in the U.S. (1923–1996) using the logistic diffusion model, and meta-analysis of 188 different product-country combinations (1950–1992) using the Bass model
Managerial implications	New product diffusion cycles have shortened markedly over time. They need not keep doing so, depending on changes in demographic and economic trends.
Contributor	Christophe Van den Bulte, University of Pennsylvania
References	Van den Bulte, Christophe (2000), "New Product Diffusion Acceleration: Measurement and Analysis." *Marketing Science* 19 (4), 366–80
	Van den Bulte, Christophe (2002), "Want to Know How Diffusion Speed Varies across Countries and Products? Try Using a Bass Model." *PDMA Visions* 26 (4), 12–5
	Van den Bulte, Christophe, and Stefan Stremersch (2004), "Social Contagion and Income Heterogeneity in New Product Diffusion: A Meta-Analytic Test." *Marketing Science* 23 (4), 530–44

Social Influence on Consumer Demand

Demand for hedonic products is strongly driven by other consumers' choices. Compared to conditions without social information, if social influence is displayed, market concentration increases: the Gini coefficient is significantly higher with respect to music choice (.220 > .147), movie interest (.105 >.088), and fashion consideration (.178 > .155). Even small and coincidental agglomerations of demand can attract cascades of customers, which reduces the predictability of market outcomes.

Evidence base	Social macro-experiment (1,143 participants) comparing independent and social influence settings across three product categories (music, movies, and scarves)
Managerial implications	On the aggregate, social influence results in herding effects. This increases demand for popular products whereas unpopular products become even less popular. As sales ranks become increasingly widespread in social networks, low market share positioning becomes less attractive while profitability of market leadership is further increased. This forces the majority of companies to monitor sales ranks closely and update demand predictions accordingly.
Contributors	Olaf Maecker, Nadja S. Grabenströer, Michel Clement, and Mark Heitmann, University of Hamburg
References	Maecker, Olaf, Nadja S. Grabenströer, Michel Clement, and Mark Heitmann (2013), "Charts and Demand: Empirical Generalizations on Social Influence." *International Journal of Research in Marketing* 30 (4), 429–31

Salganik, Matthew J., Peter S. Dodds, and Duncan J. Watts (2006), "Experimental Study of Inequality and Unpredictability in an Artificial Cultural Market." *Science* 311, 854–6

Seeding Strategies for Viral Marketing

Seeding targets in viral marketing should include two kinds of people that perform equally well: (1) "hubs", i.e., people with a high number of connections to others and (2) "bridges", i.e., people who connect two otherwise unconnected parts of the network. Both seeding strategies perform between 39% and 100% better than a random seeding strategy. The measure of "degree centrality" identifies "hubs" and "betweenness centrality" identifies "bridges".

Evidence base	Two field experiments with 120 and 1,380 participants and an empirical study of a referral program that involved 208,829 customers of a telecommunication company
Managerial implications	Seeding to (1) well-connected people ("high degree seeding") and (2) people who connect two otherwise unconnected parts of the network ("high betweenness seeding") performs best. Sociometric measures such as degree centrality and betweenness centrality are very important metrics for viral marketing and should be used more often for targeting purposes.
Contributor	Bernd Skiera, Goethe University Frankfurt
Reference	Hinz, Oliver, Bernd Skiera, Christian Barrot, and Jan Becker (2011), "An Empirical Comparison of Seeding Strategies for Viral Marketing." *Journal of Marketing* 75 (November), 55–71

8

Product Innovation

Innovation Generation

The key drivers of innovation and their effect sizes are past innovation (effect size = .47), openness to change (effect size = .36), presence of innovation champions (effect size = .29), customer orientation (effect size = .25), intelligence generation (effect size = .23), and extent of professionalism (effect size = .23). Innovation drives firm performance on average (effect size = .09), while radical innovation has a more significant effect on firm performance (effect size = .25), and incremental innovation has a much smaller effect (effect size = .07).

Evidence base	Meta-analysis of 273 prior effect sizes from 187 studies and a sample of 337,470 observations from the period 1970–2007
Managerial implications	Innovation in firms is driven by a history of innovation, organizational resources, processes, and cultural factors. Resources such as past innovation, diversification, and network relationships, taken together, explain the majority of the variance in innovation generation. Furthermore, an organization's motivation to innovate (i.e., customer and competitor orientation, and openness to change) are also key drivers of innovation generation.
Contributors	Leslie Vincent, Eastern Kentucky University, Sundar Bharadwaj, Emory University, and Goutam Challagalla, Georgia Institute of Technology

Reference Vincent, Leslie, Sundar Bharadwaj, and Goutam Challagalla (2008), "Antecedents, Consequences, and the Mediating Role of Innovation Generation." Lexington, Kentucky: University of Kentucky, Gatton College of Business and Economics, Working Paper

Product Innovation

There is a U-shaped relation between the degree of newness of a new packaged good product and its success in the marketplace. Products of intermediate newness systematically generate a lower purchase rate during the first year after introduction compared to incrementally new products and true innovations.

Evidence base	Over 500 new product introductions in foods, beverages, personal care, and household care in France, Germany, Spain, the Netherlands, and the U.K.
Managerial implications	Beware of compromises in the new-product development process, which often lead to products that are stuck in the middle. Moderately novel products typically are not much higher in relative advantage compared to incrementally new products, while not much lower in complexity than really new innovations.
Contributor	Jan-Benedict E.M. Steenkamp, University of North Carolina at Chapel Hill
References	Gielens, Katrijn, and Jan-Benedict E.M. Steenkamp (2007), "Drivers of Consumer Acceptance of New Packaged Goods: An Investigation across Products and Countries." *International Journal of Research in Marketing* 24 (2), 97–111
	Steenkamp, Jan-Benedict E.M., and Katrijn Gielens (2003), "Consumer and Market Drivers of the Trial Probability of New Consumer Packaged Goods." *Journal of Consumer Research* 30 (3), 368–84

New Product Trial

Several consumer traits predict how likely consumers are to try a new product. Consumer innovativeness has the strongest positive impact on trial probability (relative effect size $s = .23$), followed by usage intensity ($s = .12$) and income ($s = .11$). Consumers who are susceptible to peer influences have a lower trial probability and tend to delay trial ($s = .06$). Market mavenism, a characteristic often mentioned in the context of new products, does not have an overall significant impact. However, some elements of marketing strategy can influence these results as follows:

- The effect of *advertising* is stronger for consumers who score high on market mavenism, and weaker for consumers that score high on innovativeness. Advertising also lessens the negative effect of peer influence.

- The effect of *feature* and *displays* is stronger for consumers who rate high on innovativeness, market mavenism, and usage intensity.

- The effect of the new product's *novelty* (newness) is stronger for consumers who score high on innovativeness and have higher incomes. Product newness also diminishes the positive effect of usage intensity and reinforces the negative impact of peer influence.

- The positive effect of brand strength is stronger for consumers who score high on market mavenism and usage intensity.

Evidence base	239 new product introductions in the consumer packaged goods industry in the Netherlands

Managerial implications	Consumer characteristics such as innovativeness, usage intensity, and income offer an actionable basis for segmentation and targeted marketing efforts. These traits can be assessed a priori rather than ex post. Consumers can then be classified according to their scores before new-product introduction, which helps firms decide whom to target and which marketing instruments to use in their launch strategy.
Contributor	Katrijn Gielens, University of North Carolina at Chapel Hill
Reference	Steenkamp, Jan-Benedict E.M., and Katrijn Gielens (2003), "Consumer and Market Drivers of the Trial Probability of New Consumer Packaged Goods." *Journal of Consumer Research* 30 (3), 368–84

Competition and New Product Acceptance

New product acceptance is systematically affected by the competitive environment. Consumer acceptance is higher in less concentrated, less heavily promoted, and less heavily advertised categories, and in categories with more intense competition on innovation. Competitive conduct is much more important than competitive structure: the average relative effect size of market concentration is .072, but that of competitive conduct is .509. Thus, competitive conduct shapes 50% of the total effect, either by itself, or in combination with product factors.

Negative competitive effects can be significantly reduced by variables under the control of the firm, viz., brand reputation and product newness. Overall, product newness dampens the impact of competitors' price promotion intensity and new product introduction intensity. These two moderating effects of product newness each explain up to 10% of the total effect of the drivers of new product success. Brand reputation has a softening effect on the impact of competitive advertising intensity, accounting for 6% of the total effect.

Evidence base	Over 300 product introductions in the consumer packaged goods industry in four countries (France, Germany, Spain, and the U.K.)
Managerial implications	Insight into the effects of the competitive environment is important in order to develop realistic marketing plans and sales targets. However, the firm introducing the new product does not have to consider competitive influences as completely beyond their control, as product newness and brand strength can be used to successfully counter negative competitive effects.

Contributor	Katrijn Gielens, University of North Carolina at Chapel Hill
Reference	Gielens, Katrijn, and Jan-Benedict E.M. Steenkamp (2007), "Drivers of Consumer Acceptance of New Packaged Goods: An Investigation Across Products and Countries." *International Journal of Research in Marketing* 24 (2), 97–111

New Product Announcements and Stock Prices

The stock market reaction to a product-innovation announcement is, on average, approximately .5% abnormal return (return over and above the expected stock return for the announcing firm).

Evidence base	1,101 *Wall Street Journal* new product announcements, 105 product announcements in the Predicast F&S Index database, and 5,481 announcements from Factiva, Lexis Nexis, and company websites
Managerial implications	All else equal, the market value of firms increases following the announcement of introduction of a new product. This generalization does not suggest that any incremental innovation is a positive net present value project. Rather, new products that are significant enough to warrant a press release by the parent firm are, on average, viewed by investors as increasing the future cash flows of the firm.
	While abnormal returns to announcements of new products in high tech industries have typically been shown to be higher than .5%, studies across multiple industries (Chaney, Devinney, and Winer 1991; Sood and Tellis 2009) have consistently demonstrated positive abnormal returns following such announcements.
Contributor	Alina Sorescu, Texas A&M University
References	Chaney, Paul K., Timothy M. Devinney, and Russell S. Winer (1991), "The Impact of New Product Introductions on the Market Value of Firms." *Journal of Business* 64 (4), 573–610
	Lee, Hun, Ken G. Smith, Curtis M. Grimm, and August Schomburg (2000), "Timing, Order and Durability of New Product Advantages with Imitation." *Strategic Management Journal* 21 (1), 23–30

Sood, Ashish, and Gerard J. Tellis (2009), "Do Innovations Really Pay Off? Total Stock Market Returns to Innovation." *Marketing Science* 28 (3), 442–56

Long-term Effect of Innovation on Firm Value

The long-term (one-year window) effect of innovation on firm stock market value is significantly positive and is greater for radical than for incremental innovations.

Evidence base	399 innovations introduced by 6 automobile firms; 22,532 innovations introduced by 153 consumer packaged goods firms
Managerial implications	All else equal, innovation has a persistent, long-term positive effect on firm stock market value and this effect is greater for radical than for incremental innovations.
Contributor	Alina Sorescu, Texas A&M University
References	Pauwels, Koen, Jorge Silva-Risso, Shuba Srinivasan, and Dominique M. Hanssens (2004), "New Products, Sales Promotions, and Firm Value: The Case of the Automobile Industry." *Journal of Marketing* 68 (4), 142–56 Sorescu, Alina, and Jelena Spanjol (2008), "Innovation's Effect on Firm Value and Risk: Insights from Consumer Packaged Goods." *Journal of Marketing* 72 (2), 114–32

Consumer Innovation Adoption

Drivers of consumer innovation adoption differ between adoption intention and adoption behavior. Intention is higher for innovations that are more ompatible with consumer needs (the weighted average bivariate correlation is .34), are relatively advantageous (.18), more complex (.04), and involve lower uncertainty (−.44). Behavior is stronger for innovations with lower perceived complexity (−.23), higher relative advantage (.25), and compatibility (.13). The effect of complexity may vary by product type. Adopter demographics explain little variance in adoption intention and behavior, whereas adopter psychographics (e.g., innovativeness, product involvement, opinion leadership) are influential in both stages.

Evidence base	Meta-analysis of 77 studies
Managerial implications	As consumers weigh evaluative criteria differently when expressing innovation purchase intention compared to actual behavior, market research tapping attitudes and purchase intentions for new products may be poor predictors of innovation success. To stimulate adoption intention, marketers should make clear who is likely to benefit most from an innovation and why, and consumers' perceived uncertainty regarding use of the innovation should be reduced.
	Product features can trigger and enhance interest in the innovation, thus stimulating adoption intention. However, this should be done with caution as product complexity is an important barrier to adoption. To increase adoption behavior, marketers should relate the innovation to context-specific use situations that enable consumers to evaluate use consequences of the innovation and thus assess its particular benefits.

Contributor	Ruud T. Frambach, VU University Amsterdam
Reference	Arts, Joep W.C., Ruud T. Frambach, and Tammo H.A. Bijmolt (2011), "Generalizations on Consumer Innovation Adoption: A Meta-Analysis on the Drivers of Intention and Behavior." *International Journal of Research in Marketing* 28 (2), 134–44

Returns to Innovation by Stage of Development

1. Total market returns to an innovation project are about 13 times greater than the returns to an average event in the innovation project.

2. Of the three innovation activities—initiation, development, and commercialization—returns to the development activities are consistently the highest across and within categories. Returns to launch are the lowest.

3. Returns to initiation occur about five years ahead of launch.

4. Returns to negative events are higher in absolute value than those to positive events.

5. Returns are consistently higher for small firms than for large firms and for those that focus on a few rather than many technologies.

Evidence base	5,481 announcements from 69 firms in five industries from 1977 to 2006
Managerial implications	1. Financial markets respond promptly and substantially to announcements about innovation at all stages of the innovation project.
	2. Firms cannot game the system by over-announcing or issuing multiple announcements of a single event. Moreover, the first announcement of a project is no more important than later announcements.
	3. Firms should be cautious not to exaggerate progress in their innovation projects or to resort to vaporware, as the absolute value of a negative announcement is greater than that for a positive announcement.

4. Returns are highest for developmental activities. Thus, it is important that firms exploit the progress in development by fully announcing all such developments.

5. When announcing innovations, small firms do not seem to suffer any disadvantage relative to large firms.

Contributors	Ashish Sood, Georgia State University, and Gerard J. Tellis, University of Southern California
Reference	Sood, Ashish, and Gerard J. Tellis (2009), "Do Innovations Really Payoff? Total Stock Market Returns to Innovation." *Marketing Science* 28 (3), 442–56

Firm Innovativeness and Performance Outcomes

- Innovativeness has direct positive effects on financial position ($r = .14$) and firm value ($r = .16$).

- Firm innovativeness indirectly affects firm value through its effects on market position and financial position.

- Positive effects of firm innovativeness on market position and financial position are stronger for larger firms, firms that invest more in advertising, firms in high-tech industries, for innovativeness outputs, and for radical innovations.

- The innovativeness–firm value relationship is stronger for smaller firms, for firms that invest more in advertising, for firms in low-tech industries, for innovativeness inputs, innovativeness culture, and for radical innovations.

Evidence base	Meta-analysis of 153 prior studies
Managerial implications	▪ The direct impact of innovativeness on firm value is stronger than its impact through market and financial positions. Thus, investors reward innovative efforts even before the commercialization of new products. ▪ Innovativeness does not only enable a firm to increase its revenues and market share, but it also leads to the development of internal capabilities that help firms reduce the costs of operations.

- Small firms competing in low-tech industries with small advertising budgets can partially make up for their disadvantage in the marketplace by introducing radically new products, especially in Western countries. Nevertheless, these firms still receive strong investor support, despite lower revenues and profits in the marketplace.

- Large firms in high-tech industries have a natural disadvantage in leveraging innovativeness to directly increase their firm value. Managers of these firms should design communication campaigns that emphasize how well their innovative efforts pay off in terms of market position and financial position.

Contributors	Gaia Rubera, Bocconi University, and Ahmet H. Kirca, Michigan State University
Reference	Rubera, Gaia, and Ahmet H. Kirca (2012), "Firm Innovativeness and Its Performance Outcomes: A Meta-Analytic Review and Theoretical Integration." *Journal of Marketing* 76 (3), 130–47

Impact of Service Innovations

E-innovativeness (defined as the number of Internet-based service innovations introduced in a given year) has a positive direct effect on firm value (Tobin's Q). P-innovativeness (number of people-based service innovations) has no direct effect on firm value. However, in human-dominated industries, they have a positive net effect on firm value by positively influencing customer satisfaction (which in turn positively affects firm value).

Both e-innovativeness and p-innovativeness increase idiosyncratic risk. However, in human-dominated industries, this effect can indirectly be mitigated for p-innovativeness by increasing customer satisfaction (which has a negative effect on idiosyncratic risk).

Evidence base	Analysis of 1,049 service innovations over five years and more than 100 successful market-creating service innovations and hybrid innovation bundles
Managerial implications	1. Firms in human-dominated industries should consider launching p-innovations.
	2. Firms in non-human-dominated industries should more carefully proceed with p-innovations than firms in human-dominated industries.
	3. Managers in non-human-dominated industries should use a metric other than customer satisfaction as a measure of innovation success because service innovativeness has a non-significant or even negative effect on customer satisfaction.
	4. In small markets, when margins are high, firms should invest in e-innovations.
Contributors	Venkatesh Shankar, Texas A&M University, and Thomas Dotzel, McGill University

References

Berry, Leonard L., Venkatesh Shankar, Janet Parish, Susan Cadwallader, and Thomas Dotzel (2006), "Creating New Markets through Service Innovations." *Sloan Management Review* 47 (2), 56–63

Dotzel, Thomas, Venkatesh Shankar, and Leonard L. Berry (2013), "Service Innovativeness and Firm Value." *Journal of Marketing Research* 50 (2), 259–76

Shankar, Venkatesh, Leonard L. Berry, and Thomas Dotzel (2009), "A Practical Guide to Combining Products and Services." *Harvard Business Review* 87 (11), 94–9

9
Price Effects

Price Elasticity

For consumer packaged goods, the average price-to-sales elasticity at the brand level is −2.62. Price elasticities are stronger at the stock keeping unit level (−2.97) than at the brand level (−2.50) and stronger in sales models (−2.89) than in market share and choice models (−2.57). In the short run, the promotional price elasticity is larger in magnitude (−3.63) than the actual price elasticity (−2.36), but the reverse is true in the long run: −3.17 for promotional price versus −3.78 for actual price.

Price elasticities are stronger (more negative) in the introduction/growth stage than in the mature/decline stage and stronger for durables than for fast moving consumer goods, following this pattern:

	Introduction or growth stage	Mature or decline stage
Groceries, high stockpiling	−2.71	−2.60
Groceries, low stockpiling	−4.10	−2.62
Durables	−5.38	−3.81

The price elasticity for sales has become stronger (more negative) over the past half century, becoming .50 more negative every decade.

Evidence base	Meta-analysis of 1,851 price elasticities across 81 studies
Managerial implications	For consumer packaged goods, price has grown in importance as a determinant of sales since the 1950s. Over time, discounting has become more effective in boosting sales, but raising prices has an increasingly negative impact on sales. When introducing a new product category, a penetration pricing strategy (low to high) is more effective than a skimming price strategy (high to low).
Contributor	Harald J. van Heerde, Massey University
Reference	Bijmolt, Tammo H.A., Harald J. van Heerde, and Rik G.M. Pieters (2005), "New Empirical Generalizations on the Determinants of Price Elasticity." *Journal of Marketing Research* 42 (2), 141–56

Reference Price Effects

Reference price effects were found in 92% of 13 studies: 85% reported a reference price effect in brand choice, and 1 of only 2 studies of purchase incidence found an effect. The smoothing parameter for past prices in the formation of reference averages .60, implying that only one to two past prices are salient in reference price formation. The "sticker shock" elasticity to utility in brand choice is 1.3. For example, the base disutility of shelf price of a brand is increased by about 13% for every 10% positive difference between the observed price and the reference price.

Evidence base	Analysis of the results of 13 prior studies covering 20 frequently purchased product categories. Smoothing parameter and "sticker shock" elasticity are based on analysis of parameters reported in Briesch et al. (1997) for 4 product categories.
Managerial implications	Consumers react not only to competitive prices but also compare them favorably or unfavorably in relation to the prices observed on recent purchases. Managers can therefore increase the likelihood of choosing a brand by communicating the brand's price positively relative to its recent past prices.
Contributors	Tridib Mazumdar, Syracuse University, and S. P. Raj, Syracuse University
References	Bell, David R., and James M. Lattin (2000), "Looking for Loss Aversion in Scanner Panel Data: The Confounding Effect of Price Response Heterogeneity." *Marketing Science* 19 (2), 185–200
	Briesch, Richard A., Lakshman Krishnamurthi, Tridib Mazumdar, and S.P. Raj (1997), "A Comparative Analysis of Reference Price Models." *Journal of Consumer Research* 24 (2), 202–14

Mazumdar, Tridib, S.P. Raj, and Indrajit Sinha (2005), "Reference Price Research: Review and Propositions." *Journal of Marketing* 69 (4), 84–102

Effects of Pricing Periodicity

Variation in brand retail prices

- Price changes over the medium term (price cycle length of 4 to 13 weeks) and the long term (greater than 13-week cycles) explain most of the variation in supermarket prices of consumer packaged goods. Short-term promotional price changes (2- to 4-week cycles), such as deals followed by return to regular price, explain the least amount of variation in supermarket prices.

- The dominant frequency of price variation varies systematically with brand and category factors. For example, greater purchase frequency increases the dominant frequency of price variation.

Covariation in retail prices across brands

- Price covariation occurs in multiple frequencies, usually not coinciding with the sample frequency of the data. Like price variation, this depends on brand and category factors.

- Discounts are often staggered across brands whereas regular price changes are often concurrent. Therefore, it is possible to observe no price covariation in aggregate data even when there is substantial price covariation at different frequencies.

Evidence base	Time series analysis across 35 grocery categories, 400 weeks, and a total of 166 brands
Managerial implications	Competitive price interactions depend on the planning cycle of managers and are often obscured when mixed together. Given most models and insights confound regular and discount price changes, managers should consider each factor separately.

Contributors	Bart Bronnenberg, Tilburg University, and Carl Mela, Duke University
Reference	Bronnenberg, Bart J., Carl F. Mela, and William Boulding (2006), "The Periodicity of Pricing." *Journal of Marketing Research* 43 (3), 477–93

Cross-price Impact: Neighborhood Price Effects

In grocery products, brands that are closer to each other in price have greater cross-price effects than brands that are priced farther apart. In particular, brands that are closest to each other in price have an average absolute cross-price effect of .090, while brands that are priced farther apart (fourth closest in price) have an average absolute cross-price effect of .043. This phenomenon is called the "neighborhood price effect." Absolute cross-price effect is measured as the change in market share (percentage) points of a target brand when a competing brand's price changes by 1% of the category price.

Evidence base	Meta-analysis of 1,060 cross-price effects on 280 brands from 19 different grocery product categories
Managerial implications	All else equal, brand managers should carefully monitor the discounts of their closely priced neighboring brands and, if necessary, provide offsetting discounts to avoid loss of sales.
Contributor	Raj Sethuraman, Southern Methodist University
References	Sethuraman, Raj, V. Srinivasan, and Doyle Kim (1999), "Asymmetric and Neighborhood Cross-Price Effects: Some Empirical Generalizations." *Marketing Science* 18 (1), 23–41

Cross-price Impact: Asymmetric Price Effects

The average cross-price elasticity of a higher-priced national brand's price cut on a lower-priced store brand's market share is .48, which is higher than the average cross-price elasticity of a lower-priced store brand's price cut on a higher-priced national brand's market share (.34). This phenomenon is called the "asymmetric price effect." However, the average absolute cross-price effect of a higher-priced national brand's price cut on a lower-priced store brand's market share is .07, which is not different from the average absolute cross-price effect of a lower-priced store brand's price cut on the share of the higher-priced national brand (.072).

Evidence base	Meta-analysis of 210 cross-price effects from 105 national brand–store brand pairs
Managerial implications	Conventional belief holds that national brand price cuts hurt store brand sales more than the reverse. This belief implies that national brands have a greater incentive to discount to take share away from store brands than vice versa. However, the conventional belief holds only when cross-price effects are measured in terms of elasticities but not when they are measured in absolute cross-price effects. Therefore, we cannot conclude that national brands have greater incentive to discount to garner store brand sales than vice versa.
Contributor	Raj Sethuraman, Southern Methodist University
References	Blattberg, Robert C., and Kenneth J. Wisniewski (1989), "Price-Induced Patterns of Competition." *Marketing Science* 8 (4), 291–309

Sethuraman, Raj, V. Srinivasan, and Doyle Kim (1999), "Asymmetric and Neighborhood Cross-Price Effects: Some Empirical Generalizations." *Marketing Science* 18 (1), 23–41

Cross-price Impact: Asymmetric Share Effects

The average absolute cross-price effect of a low-share brand's price cut on the market share of a high-share brand is .069, which is greater than the average absolute cross-price effect of a high-share brand's price cut on the market share of a low-share brand (.043). This phenomenon is called the "asymmetric share effect."

Evidence base	Meta-analysis of 1,060 cross-price effects on 280 brands from 19 different grocery product categories
Managerial implications	All else equal, manufacturers of low-share brands would have a greater incentive to discount because they can attract a larger pool of consumers.
Contributor	Raj Sethuraman, Southern Methodist University
Reference	Sethuraman, Raj, and V. Srinivasan (2002), "The Asymmetric Share Effect: An Empirical Generalization on Cross-Price Effects." *Journal of Marketing Research* 39 (3), 379–86

Private Label Margins

In grocery products, the gross percentage profit margin per unit received by the retailer on the store brand is greater than the retailer's percentage margin on the national brand. One gross margin estimate is 34% for store brands and 24% for national brands. Gross percent margin is the profit contribution computed as a percent of brand price = [(price − variable cost) × 100/price].

Evidence base	Compilation of six academic and industry studies
Managerial implications	The higher gross percentage margin for store brands does not imply that retailers should promote their store brands, nor does it necessarily imply that manufacturers should close the percent margin gap by reducing their wholesale prices. Retailers and manufacturers should consider unit dollar contribution margin (price − variable cost) and profitability per square foot of retail space when making their price and promotion decisions.
Contributor	Raj Sethuraman, Southern Methodist University
References	Sethuraman, Raj (2006), "Private-Label Marketing Strategies in Packaged Goods: Management Beliefs and Research Insights." Cambridge, Mass.: Marketing Science Institute, Report No. 06–108
	Sethuraman, Raj (2009), "Assessing the External Validity of Analytical Results from National Brand and Store Brand Competition Models." *Marketing Science* 28 (4), 759–81

Price Stickiness

While changes in demand, cost, and competitive prices do have an effect, past-pricing patterns are the main driver of retail price variation over time (57%). Such price stickiness is related to lower retailer profitability.

Evidence base	24 categories in Dominick's Finer Foods (http://research.chicagobooth.edu/marketing/databases/dominicks/) and 43 categories in Denver (provided by AC Nielsen)
Managerial implications	While adjusting prices to changes in demand is associated with higher retailer gross margins, past-price dependence has been linked to lower margins. Retailers' reliance on past prices also has implications for manufacturers. For example, past-price dependence is stronger for smaller brands, making it harder for manufacturers to achieve high levels of trade deal pass-through. More research is needed to quantify the cost of demand-based pricing and to develop strategies to reduce it.
Contributors	Vincent Nijs, University of California, San Diego, Koen Pauwels, Özyeğin University, and Shuba Srinivasan, Boston University
References	Nijs, Vincent R., Shuba Srinivasan, and Koen Pauwels (2007), "Retail-Price Drivers and Retailer Profits." *Marketing Science* 26 (4), 473–87
	Srinivasan, Shuba, Koen Pauwels, and Vincent Nijs (2008), "Demand-Based Pricing Versus Past-Price Dependence: A Cost-Benefit Analysis." *Journal of Marketing* 72 (2), 15–27

Effectiveness of Within-Store vs. Between-Store Semantic Price Cues

Within-store semantic price cues (e.g., "regular price versus sale price"), relative to between-store semantic price cues (e.g., "compare at, sale price"), enhance customer evaluations when the consumer shops in stores, but the reverse effect arises when the consumer shops from home.

Evidence base	Meta-analysis of seven studies (in-store effects) and eight studies (at-home effects)
Managerial implications	Consumer price sensitivity varies by consumers' location: effective communication of price promotions is different for consumers exposed at home vs. in-store. While at home, shoppers are more sensitive to advertised price promotion differences across stores, whereas in-store, they react more to price changes over time.
Contributors	Dhruv Grewal, Babson College, Anne L. Roggeveen, Babson College, and Joan Lindsey-Mullikin, California Polytechnic State University
Reference	Grewal, Dhruv, Anne L. Roggeveen, and Joan Lindsey-Mullikin (2014), "Contingent Effects of Semantic Price Cues." *Journal of Retailing* 90 (June), 198–205

10

Brands and Brand Loyalty

Brand Price Premium

For grocery products, consumers will pay a price premium for national brands even when the quality of the national brands and the store brands is the same. This premium is called the image premium or reputation premium. Price premium is measured as [price willing to pay for national brand – price of store brand] expressed as a percent of national brand price. The average image premium has been estimated at 26%.

Evidence base	20 grocery products, 132 consumer and 78 grocery products, aggregate consumer reports data
Managerial implications	National brand managers can maintain and increase the image premium through advertising and other marketing activities that enhance perceptions of brand equity. Retailers may need to charge a lower price for their store brands (that is, maintain a minimum price differential between national brands and store brands) even if there is no significant perceived quality difference between the two brands.
Contributor	Raj Sethuraman, Southern Methodist University
References	Apelbaum, Eidan, Eitan Gerstner, and Prasad Naik (2003), "The Effects of Expert Quality Evaluations versus Brand Name on Price Premiums." *Journal of Product and Brand Management* 12 (3), 154–65

Sethuraman, Raj (2000), "What Makes Consumers Pay More for National Brands Than for Store Brands: Image or Quality?" Cambridge, Mass.: Marketing Science Institute Report No. 00–110

Sethuraman, Raj (2003), "Measuring National Brands' Equity over Store Brands." *Review of Marketing Science* 1 (2), 1–26

Private Labels and Store Loyalty

There is an inverted U-shaped relationship between consumers' private label share in a chain and their behavioral loyalty to that chain. Chain loyalty first increases with private label share, but the effect turns negative at private label shares around 35–40%.

Evidence base	Consumer packaged goods: analysis of shoppers at two major retail chains in the U.S. and two major retail chains in the Netherlands
Managerial implications	Private label use increases store loyalty but only up to a point. Beyond that, the effect can be negative, so retailers must have a good balance of national and store brands in order to optimize store traffic, sales, and loyalty.
Contributor	Kusum Ailawadi, Dartmouth College
References	Ailawadi, Kusum, and Bari Harlam (2004), "An Empirical Analysis of the Determinants of Retail Margins: The Role of Store-Brand Share." *Journal of Marketing* 68 (1), 147–65
	Ailawadi, Kusum L., Koen Pauwels, and Jan-Benedict E.M. Steenkamp (2008), "Private-Label Use and Store Loyalty." *Journal of Marketing* 72 (6), 19–30

Determinants of Store Brand Share

Store brand shares are higher among households with lower *income* ($E = -.31$, $z = -19.8$), larger *household size* ($E = .11$, $z = 3.1$) and higher *education* ($E = .56$, $z = 19.2$).

Consumers will purchase more store brands if those consumers are more *price sensitive* ($E = .80$, $z = 21.5$), less *quality sensitive* ($E = -1$, $z = -6.5$) and more *familiar with store brands* ($E = .78$, $z = 33.0$). They will also purchase more store brands if they perceive that the *store brand quality* is higher ($E = .69$, $z = 35.2$) and *quality variation* is lower ($E = -.50$, $z = -9$), have a *positive image of store brands* ($E = .79$, $z = 9.7$), and think that store brands are not *risky* ($E = -.55$, $z = -24.4$).

Consumers will purchase more store brands if their *shopping frequency* is higher ($E = .67$, $z = 10.6$). There is a positive relationship between store brand share and *store loyalty* ($E = .67$, $z = 8.0$), but not with shopping basket expenditure ($E = -.40$, $z = -.67$).

Store brand share is lower when there are more *national brands* ($E = -.87$, $z = -10.8$) and when the *price competition in the category* among national brands is higher ($E = -1$, $z = -5.24$). Store brand share is higher when *concentration among national brands* is lower ($E = -.80$, $z = -5.1$) but *retail concentration* ($E = .35$, $z = 10.5$) is higher.

Store brand share is higher when *price differential between national brand and store brand* is higher ($E = .18$, $z = 6.18$) and when the *retail promotion of store brands* is higher ($E = .42$, $z = 15.2$). But store brand share is lower when *national brand retail promotion* is higher ($E = -.40$, $z = -23.9$) and *national brand advertising* is higher ($E = -.37$, $z = -8.67$).

Evidence base	Meta-analysis of 54 studies
Managerial implications	Lack of education, lack of store brand familiarity, and lack of positive store brand image are the reasons why lower-income consumers are less prone to purchasing store brands. This finding has implications for retailers and public policy makers interested in educating and making low-income consumers familiar with store brands and making them recognize store brand quality and value.
	The future of store brands and national brands will continue to depend on how retailers and national brand marketers manage perceptions, potentially signaling the growing role of store brand advertising in coming years. Furthermore, perceived store brand quality has a stronger effect on store brand share than the national brand–store brand price differential, confirming the notion that consumers seek value when purchasing store brands without compromising much on quality.
	Retailers interested in boosting store brand share may want to focus on stimulating shopping frequency.
	Item proliferation can limit store brand growth and highlights the importance of product assortment for retailers. Retailers should leverage national brand–national brand price competition for profits in some categories rather than engaging in national brand–store brand competition to promote store brand share.
	Retailers will have to re-allocate more substantial shares of their marketing budget to non-price promotional tools in order to maintain and grow store brand shares in the future.

Contributors	Katrijn Gielens, University of North Carolina, and Raj Sethuraman, Southern Methodist University
References	Sethuraman, Raj, and Katrijn Gielens (2014), "Determinants of Store Brand Share." *Journal of Retailing* 90 (2), 141–53

Brand Loyalty Evolution

	Brand loyalty for consumer packaged goods is not systematically declining over time, nor is the short-run variability around a brand's mean loyalty level.
Evidence base	Time-series analysis on monthly or bi-monthly loyalty estimates for 92 brands from 21 frequently purchased consumer goods categories over one to two years
Managerial implications	Managers are often concerned about recurring claims that brand loyalty is gradually eroding. While managers should not become complacent, these claims are largely exaggerated, especially for market share leaders.
Contributors	Marnik G. Dekimpe, Tilburg University and Catholic University of Leuven, and Jan-Benedict E.M. Steenkamp, University of North Carolina at Chapel Hill
Reference	Dekimpe, Marnik G., Jan-Benedict E.M. Steenkamp, Martin Mellens, and Piet Vanden Abeele (1997), "Decline and Variability in Brand Loyalty." *International Journal of Research in Marketing* 14 (5), 405–20

Private Label Quality

For grocery products, a decrease in the perceived quality differential between a national brand and store brand increases the store brand's unit market share. According to one estimate, a 1% decrease in perceived quality differential between national and store brands increases store brand market share by .3%. This represents a 1.74% increase from the average store brand unit market share of 17.2%.

Evidence base	Estimate based on data from 210 grocery product categories; generalization based on a compilation of 16 academic and industry studies
Managerial implications	Quality has been found to be an important consideration for private label purchases (sometimes even more important than price). Retailers should generally emphasize quality in their product development and promotion of private labels. Manufacturers should attempt to differentiate their national brands on quality.
Contributor	Raj Sethuraman, Southern Methodist University
References	Hoch, Stephen J., and Shumeet Banerji (1993), "When Do Private Labels Succeed?" *Sloan Management Review* 34 (4), 57–67
	Sethuraman, Raj (2006), "Private-Label Marketing Strategies in Packaged Goods: Management Beliefs and Research Insights." Cambridge, Mass.: Marketing Science Institute Report No. 06–108

National Brand and Private Label Product Introductions

- Products introduced by leading national brands ($z = 2.82$), standard private labels ($z = 2.38$), and premium private labels ($z = 2.16$) are more likely to increase category sales than products introduced by follower national brands ($p > .10$) or economy private labels ($p > .10$).

- New products introduced by leader ($z = 2.02$) as well as follower national brands ($z = 3.55$) more often boost own share.

- New products impact rival shares ($z = -13.47$), with the exception of economy private label launches. National brands tend to hurt rival national brands more often than private labels and only the leading national brand is likely to steal share from all three private label tiers. Moreover, standard private labels tend to be harmed less often ($p > .10$) by rival new products, unless introduced by the leading national brand ($z = -1.98$).

- Private labels are more likely to be affected by a national brand that maintains a large price gap and offers new products with new intrinsic or usage benefits.

- To fight economy private labels successfully, national brands have to maintain a smaller price gap, while offering products that focus less on intrinsic and usage benefits.

Evidence base — Over 300 national brand and private label new product introductions in the consumer packaged goods industry in the U.K.

Managerial implications	Manipulating the right mix of new product attributes and brand positioning can help national brands reduce the inroads in private label competitors' market positions. While the price gap plays no role in influencing a new product's impact on rival national brands, it does reinforce the competitive impact of new products when taking on private labels.

New products offering substantially new, intrinsic benefits are most effective and even more so when fighting private labels rather than national brands. This competitive effect is especially strong when facing premium private labels and plays a more moderate role when facing economy private labels. In contrast, private labels can hardly be hurt by new products that offer new, extrinsic benefits. Still, continued innovation in packaging can become a competitive tool to fight premium private labels.

Finally, new products that offer no new intrinsic or extrinsic benefits can impact standard and premium private labels, but weaken the competitive impact relative to economy private label rivals. This will be even more so, if that new product is offered by a national brand that maintains a relatively small price premium. |
| *Contributor* | Katrijn Gielens, University of North Carolina at Chapel Hill |
| *Reference* | Gielens, Katrijn (2012), "New Products: The Antidote to Private Label Growth?" *Journal of Marketing Research* 49 (3), 408–23 |

Private Labels and National Brands

Widespread availability of private labels and the price gap with national brands are the two most important drivers of private label success. For national brands, the most effective weapons in the battle against private labels are innovation and advertising, with the former having the strongest effect. A strategy relying on innovation is effective around the world. However, advertising is not effective in smaller countries. Price promotions can be effective to fight private labels but the effect is context-specific.

Evidence base	Market share of private labels for 23 countries in Asia, Europe, Latin America, and North America, covering 3–5 years for, on average, 54 CPG categories per country
Managerial implications	*For retailers:* While the objective quality of private labels is often close to that of national brands, consumer perceptions have not caught up with this. Retailers need to close the perceived quality gap, using in-store signs, employing aggressive "brand challenge" strategies pioneered by U.S. retailer Publix (buy-one-national brand, get-Publix-brand-free promotion), and others. It is also important to deliver consistent quality across the entire range of products offered, something that most retailers have not achieved. But maintaining the price gap remains crucial. The market for price-equivalent private labels remains small. Hence, some strategies to over-complicate private label assortments may go too far. Finally, widespread private label availability per se in the shopping area of a consumer has a strong effect on its success. Yet, availability differs dramatically across categories and countries.

For brand manufacturers: Manufacturers need to innovate more, not less—which is exactly opposite to what national brands have been doing in the last decade. Further, advertising remains a highly effective weapon against private labels in larger countries, where economies of scale and scope still favor brand manufacturers. Promotion strategies should be left to local managers.

Contributor	Jan-Benedict E.M. Steenkamp, University of North Carolina at Chapel Hill
References	Kumar, Nirmalya, and Jan-Benedict E.M. Steenkamp (2007), *Private Label Strategy: How to Meet the Store Brand Challenge.* Cambridge: Mass.: Harvard Business School Press
	Steenkamp, Jan-Benedict E.M., and Inge Geyskens (2014), "Manufacturer and Retailer Strategies to Impact Store Brand Share: Global Integration, Local Adaptation, and Worldwide Learning." *Marketing Science* 33 (1), 6–26

11

Price Promotions

Retail Promotion Pass-Through

For manufacturers who provide trade promotion funds and receive promotion spending by retailers, the median pass-through rate by retailers is 65–75%. Pass-through is greater than 100% for 10–25% of manufacturers. Pass-through is higher for large-share manufacturers and in high-sales product categories.

Evidence base	Consumer packaged goods: Analysis of promotion spending by two U.S. retail chains across multiple product categories (25 categories sold by one chain and all categories sold by the other chain)
Managerial implications	There is wide variation in pass-through rates across product categories and across manufacturers. Manufacturers must understand the drivers of retail promotion decisions and design win-win trade promotions that are most likely to be passed through.
Contributor	Kusum Ailawadi, Dartmouth College
References	Ailawadi, Kusum, and Bari Harlam (2009), "Findings—Retailer Promotion Pass-Through: A Measure, Its Magnitude, and Its Determinants." *Marketing Science* 28 (4), 782–91
	Besanko, David, Jean-Pierre Dubé, and Sachin Gupta (2005), "Own-Brand and Cross-Brand Retail Pass-Through." *Marketing Science* 24 (1), 123–37

Channel Pass-Through of Trade Promotions

For one consumer packaged goods category, pass-through elasticities average .71 for the wholesaler, .59 for the retailer, and .42 for the channel. As an example, a 10% reduction in manufacturer price would result in a 4.2% consumer price reduction.

Evidence base	Two years of data on prices, shipments, sales, and promotions for the distribution channel (i.e., manufacturer, wholesaler, and retailer) in a major consumer packaged goods category in over 30 U.S. states
Managerial implications	Manufacturers and retailers have debated the level of trade-deal pass-through for decades. The profitability of manufacturer and wholesaler deals can be improved by utilizing detailed effectiveness estimates. For example, a manufacturer using an inclusive trade-deal strategy might offer a 10% off-invoice deal to all retailers on every product. This strategy would decrease manufacturer and wholesaler profits for 56% of product/store combinations, while retailers would experience a profit boost in 96% of cases. Manufacturers and wholesalers can avoid unprofitable trade deals for specific products and retailers by utilizing accurate estimates of pass-through, consumer demand elasticity, and margins. Such a selective trade-deal strategy could improve deal profitability by up to 86% and reduce costs by 40%. Although total retailer profits would drop by 51%, retailers receiving deals could still see a profit boost in 95% of cases.
Contributors	Vincent Nijs, University of California, San Diego, and Kanishka Misra, University of Michigan
Reference	Nijs, Vincent R., Kanishka Misra, Eric Anderson, Karsten Hansen, and Lakshman Krishnamurthi (2009), "Channel Pass-Through of Trade Promotions." *Marketing Science* 29 (2), 1–18

Category-Demand Effects of Price Promotions

In the majority of cases (58%) price promotions significantly expand the size of a category, with a net elasticity (2.21) that is accumulated over a period of 10 weeks on average. Persistent category-demand effects of price promotions are rare (2% of cases).

Evidence base	Four years of data on 560 supermarket product categories in the Netherlands
Managerial implications	Price promotions can increase the size of the pie (category demand), not just the relative size of the slices (market share). To enhance retailer cooperation, manufacturers should demonstrate that promotions can temporarily boost demand for an entire category. Since long-run effects of price promotions are rare, retailers should focus on other marketing instruments, such as new product introductions, to achieve persistent growth.
Contributor	Vincent Nijs, University of California, San Diego
Reference	Nijs, Vincent R., Marnik G. Dekimpe, Jan-Benedict E.M. Steenkamp, and Dominique M. Hanssens (2001), "The Category-Demand Effects of Price Promotions." *Marketing Science* 20 (1), 1–22

Decomposition of Long-term Sales Promotion Effects

The *total net effect* (expressed in elasticity) of a sales promotion is positive and derives mostly from primary demand expansion (category incidence and purchase quantity), not secondary demand (brand switching). About 60% of the long-term effect is due to higher category incidence; the remaining 40% is mostly captured by brand switching for perishable products, and by increased purchase quantity for storable products. These breakdowns are different from *short-term results*, where the effect is 75% secondary demand (i.e., brand choice) and 25% primary demand (i.e., category incidence and purchase quantity). For storable products, the 25% primary demand expansion is 4% category incidence, 21% purchase quantity. For perishable products, this breakdown is 17% category incidence, 8% purchase quantity.

Evidence base	17 store-brand combinations for a perishable product category and 12 store-brand combinations for a storable category, Sioux Falls, South Dakota, 1986–1988
Managerial implications	Price promotions do not only seduce consumers to switch brands, they also induce them to buy in the category in the first place. Encouraging brand manufacturers to price promote is meaningful for retailers interested in temporary demand expansion of the category.
Contributor	Koen Pauwels, Özyeğin University
References	Bell, David R., Jeongwen Chiang, and V. Padmanabhan (1999) "The Decomposition of Promotional Response: An Empirical Generalization." *Marketing Science* 18 (4), 504–26

Gupta, Sunil (1988), "Impact of Sales Promotion on When, What and How Much to Buy." *Journal of Marketing Research* 25 (4), 342–55

Pauwels, Koen, Dominique Hanssens, and S. Siddarth (2002), "The Long-Term Effects of Price Promotions on Category Incidence, Brand Choice, and Purchase Quantity." *Journal of Marketing Research* 39 (4), 421–39

Price Promotion Elasticity

Price promotions lead to a strong temporary sales increase for the promoted brand. The average price promotion elasticity is −3.63, meaning that a 10% promotional price discount leads to a 36.3% increase in brand sales. Research based on decomposing this elasticity concludes that brand switching (brand choice elasticity) accounts for the major part of the bump (75%), whereas temporary category growth (purchase incidence and quantity elasticities) comprises the remaining 25%.

However, looking at elasticities does not give the full picture, and the opposite conclusion emerges when these results are expressed in unit sales. A promotion leads to a "bigger pie": a temporary increase in that week's sales for the entire category. At the same time, competitor brands suffer from a "smaller slice of the larger pie": a temporarily lower market share. These two counteracting forces mitigate the net loss of sales for competitor brands. As a consequence, a 100-unit promotional sales bump for a brand only leads to a 33-unit (rather than 75-unit) sales loss for competitor brands and a 67-unit (rather than 25-unit) increase in category sales during the promotional week.

Evidence base	(Re-)analysis of 173 brands across 13 CPG categories
Managerial implications	In terms of unit sales effects, brand switching is a much smaller contributor to the sales bump of a promoted brand (33%) than temporary category growth in the promotional week (67% of the bump). Thus, both for retailers and manufacturers, promotions may seem more attractive than the elasticity decomposition suggests. The caveat is that part of the temporary category growth represents consumer stockpiling.

Contributor	Harald J. van Heerde, Massey University
References	Bell, David R., Jeongwen Chiang, and V. Padmanabhan (1999), "The Decomposition of Promotional Response: An Empirical Generalization." *Marketing Science* 18 (4), 504–26
	Bijmolt, Tammo H.A., Harald J. van Heerde, Rik G.M. Pieters (2005), "New Empirical Generalizations on the Determinants of Price Elasticity." *Journal of Marketing Research* 42 (2), 141–56
	Van Heerde, Harald J., Sachin Gupta, and Dick R. Wittink (2003), "Is 75% of the Sales Promotion Bump Due to Brand Switching? No, Only 33% Is." *Journal of Marketing Research* 40 (4), 481–91

Sales Promotion Effects

Price promotions do not have permanent monetary effects for either the manufacturer or the retailer. Estimates of total (long-run) price promotion elasticities are 3.70 for brand sales, 2.30 for manufacturer revenue, .50 for category sales at the chain level, 1.40 for category sales at the national level, −.05 for retailer revenue, and −.70 for retailer margins.

Evidence base	Analysis of 25 categories in the U.S. over a seven-year period; analysis of 560 consumer product categories in the Netherlands over a four-year period
Managerial implications	The interests of manufacturers and retailers are not necessarily aligned when it comes to price promotions. Therefore, it is important for each party to scrutinize the conditions under which promotions make money and allocate their scarce marketing dollars toward such cases.
Contributor	Shuba Srinivasan, Boston University
References	Nijs, Vincent R., Marnik G. Dekimpe, Jan-Benedict E.M. Steenkamp, and Dominique M. Hanssens (2001), "The Category-Demand Effects of Price Promotions." *Marketing Science* 20 (1), 1–22
	Pauwels, Koen, and Shuba Srinivasan (2004), "Who Benefits from Store Brand Entry?" *Marketing Science* 23 (3), 364–90
	Srinivasan, Shuba, Koen Pauwels, Dominique Hanssens, and Marnik Dekimpe (2002), "Who Benefits from Price Promotions?" *Harvard Business Review* 80 (9), 22–3

Srinivasan, Shuba, Koen H. Pauwels, Dominique M. Hanssens, and Marnik G. Dekimpe (2004), "Do Promotions Benefit Manufacturers, Retailers, or Both?" *Management Science* 50 (5), 617–29

Manufacturer Sales Promotions

On average, the net long-term sales effect of a manufacturer sales promotion is 10% higher when there is retailer feature and/or display support, 6% lower when the effects of retailer category management are considered, and 10% lower when brand competitor reaction is included in the analysis.

Evidence base	Across 75 brands in 25 fast-moving consumer product categories
Managerial implications	Price reactions by brand competitors matter, but retailer decisions on category management matter even more!
Contributor	Koen Pauwels, Özyeğin University
Reference	Pauwels, Koen (2007), "How Retailer and Competitor Decisions Drive the Long-Term Effectiveness of Manufacturer Promotions for Fast Moving Consumer Goods." *Journal of Retailing* 83 (3), 297–308

12
Personal Selling

Personal Selling Impact

The average personal selling-to-sales (PS) elasticity is about .34. After correcting for methodology-induced biases, the mean corrected (PS) elasticity is .31. This means that an increase of the personal selling effort (budget) by 10% results in an increase of sales by 3.1%.

On average, products in the early stages of their life cycles exhibit higher values of PS elasticity, and vice versa. Also, on average, the PS elasticity in European market settings is higher than the PS elasticity in the U.S. Further, PS elasticity estimates from more recent studies are smaller than those from older studies.

Evidence base	Meta-analysis of 75 prior studies providing a total of 506 personal selling elasticity measures
Managerial implications	All else equal, companies should invest more in direct sales force resources when launching and establishing new products, while shifting to other means of marketing communication as products mature. Similarly, all else equal, multinational firms should invest more in personal selling efforts in European markets than in U.S. markets. The efficient ratio of personal selling expenditures to total revenues is about 12.5%. Managers can use this ratio as a decision-making benchmark while setting personal selling expenditure levels.

Contributors	Sönke Albers, Kühne Logistics University, Germany, Murali Mantrala, University of Missouri, and Shrihari Sridhar, Pennsylvania State University
Reference	Albers, Sönke, Murali K. Mantrala, and Shrihari Sridhar (2010), "A Meta-Analysis of Personal Selling Elasticities." *Journal of Marketing Research* 47 (October), 840–53

Trade Show Effectiveness

The average elasticity for booth space at trade shows is .162, for booth salespeople it is .884, and for percentage of attendees with buying plans for the types of products exhibited by the firm, it is .128. All else equal, a booth in the IT sector (computers, telecom) draws twice the traffic compared to a booth in other industry sectors (medical, food, construction, and others).

Evidence base	Analyses of 18 years of trade show data covering 50 industries, 164 shows, and nearly 400 firms
Managerial implications	Booth staffing plays a much more significant role in attracting those visitors managers really want (those who have a meaningful engagement with the category) than does the size of the booth itself. Hence, managers should focus on selecting booth staff carefully to improve their company's trade show performance.
Contributors	Srinath Gopalakrishna, University of Missouri, Shrihari Sridhar, Pennsylvania State University, and Gary L. Lilien, Pennsylvania State University
Reference	Gopalakrishna, Srinath, and Gary L. Lilien (1995), "A Three-Stage Model of Industrial Trade Show Performance." *Marketing Science* 14 (1), 22–42

13

Distribution

Distribution and Market Share

In consumer packaged goods categories, market share tends to increase with retail distribution, as measured by all commodities volume (ACV) or percent commodities volume (PCV), at an increasing rate (82% of categories), or otherwise at a linear rate (14%). The degree of convexity is greater in categories with higher revenues, greater concentration in brands' market shares, and bulky items. The convex relationship has been observed at the brand level and the stock-keeping unit level. Patterns between share and unweighted distribution have not yet been established.

Evidence base	Brand-level analyses covering 143,536 brands in 263 product categories, and stock-keeping unit (SKU)–level analyses covering 79,000 SKUs totaling more than $55 billion in annual revenue in 37 product categories
Managerial implications	Retail promotions and slotting fees garner increasing returns at higher levels of retail distribution. It is more profitable to use these funds to push a small number of SKUs to relatively high levels of distribution than to push a large number of SKUs to more moderate levels of distribution.
Contributors	Paul Farris, University of Virginia, David Reibstein, University of Pennsylvania, and Kenneth C. Wilbur, University of California, San Diego

References

Kruger, Michael W. and Brian Harper (2006), "Market Share and Product Distribution: Re-Tested and Extended" (June 5). Available at SSRN: http://ssrn.com/abstract=2157528 or http://dx.doi.org/10.2139/ssrn.2157528

Reibstein, David J., and Paul W. Farris (1995), "Market Share and Distribution: A Generalization, a Speculation, and Some Implications." *Marketing Science* 14 (3), G190–202

Wilbur, Kenneth C., and Paul W. Farris (2014), "Distribution and Market Share." *Journal of Retailing* 90 (2), 154–67

Internet Channels

The addition of an Internet channel to a firm's channel portfolio is evaluated positively, on average, by the stock market. This is partly due to the fact that this addition causes little or no inter-channel cannibalization.

Evidence base	80+ newspapers that added an Internet channel to their portfolio
Managerial implications	Managers should not unduly worry when deciding whether or not to add an Internet channel. Positive outcomes should not be taken for granted either, as the stock market reacts negatively in approximately 30% of all cases. Managers can influence the sign/size of this reaction by their entry timing and the extent of publicity given to the entry.
Contributor	Marnik G. Dekimpe, Tilburg University and Catholic University of Leuven
References	Deleersnyder, Barbara, Inge Geyskens, Katrijn Gielens, and Marnik G. Dekimpe (2002), "How Cannibalistic Is the Internet Channel? A Study of the Newspaper Industry in the United Kingdom and The Netherlands." *International Journal of Research in Marketing* 19 (4), 337–48
	Geyskens, Inge, Katrijn Gielens, and Marnik G. Dekimpe (2002), "The Market Valuation of Internet Channel Additions." *Journal of Marketing* 66 (2), 102–19

Out of Stock

	The average retail out-of-stock incidence worldwide is 8.3%. The U.S. is at the low end (7.9%), Europe is at the high end (8.6%), and the rest of the world is 8.2%. More than half of out-of-stock situations last longer than 24 hours.
Evidence base	Summary of findings from 52 studies (16 published studies and 36 proprietary studies) of 32 fast-moving consumer goods categories from 71,000 customers from 29 countries
Managerial implications	A typical retailer loses about 4% of sales due to having items out of stock. This sales loss translates into an earnings per share loss of about $.012 (1.2 cents) for the average firm in the grocery retailing sector where the average earnings per share is about $.25 (25 cents) per year. Consumer response when faced with out of stock on store shelves ranges from buy at another store (31%), substitute another brand (26%), substitute same brand but different SKU (19%), delay purchase (15%), and do not purchase (9%). Seventy to seventy-five percent of out of stock is due to retailer practices including retailer ordering, forecasting, and shelving failures.
Contributors	Thomas Gruen, University of New Hampshire, Daniel Corsten, IE Business School, Madrid, and Sundar Bharadwaj, University of Georgia
Reference	Gruen, Thomas, Daniel Corsten, and Sundar Bharadwaj (2002), "Retail Out-of-Stocks: A Worldwide Examination of Extent, Causes, and Consumer Responses." Arlington, Va.: Food Marketing Institute and Grocery Manufacturers of America

Shelf Space Elasticity

The average shelf space-to-sales elasticity is .17. It varies across product categories, with the lowest estimates for commodities (.02), followed by staples (.13) and the highest estimates for impulse buys (.21). Shelf space increases results in greater elasticity estimates than shelf space reduction. Store size moderates the effect of product characteristics on shelf space elasticity: in large stores, the difference between elasticities for brand versus category is greater than in small stores.

Evidence base	Meta-analysis of 1,268 estimates of shelf space elasticities from 57 different store contexts
Managerial implications	Retailers should apply shelf space variation primarily for impulse buys and not necessarily for commodities. Small percentages of shelf space variations are more useful than large variations. Retailers benefit if they increase space for brands or categories and then cut back systematically. Larger stores should particularly focus on shelf variations at the category level.
Contributor	Martin Eisend, European University Viadrina Frankfurt
Reference	Eisend, Martin (2014), "Shelf Space Elasticity: A Meta-analysis." *Journal of Retailing* 90 (2), 168–81

Multichannel Customers: Monetary Value

Multichannel customers who buy in multiple categories provide the highest monetary value. This monetary value is the highest for hedonic products. Multichannel customers are more responsive to marketing mailers.

Evidence base	Purchase and marketing information in a syndicated database of 96 million customers of 750 retailers across 22 product categories over a four-year period; transaction and marketing data across channels of over a million customers of a large shoe and accessory firm over a two-year period; attitudinal, behavioral, and marketing data of the insurance industry over a 42-month period
Managerial implications	1. Retail firms that sell multiple product categories (e.g., mass merchandisers) should induce multichannel customers to buy more by investing in all the channels.
	2. Specialty retailers of hedonic products could incent their single-channel customers to shop in other channels because multichannel shoppers provide the highest monetary value for such products.
Contributors	Venkatesh Shankar, Texas A&M University, and Tarun Kushwaha, University of North Carolina at Chapel Hill
References	Kushwaha, Tarun, and Venkatesh Shankar (2013), "Are Multichannel Customers Really More Valuable? The Moderating Effects of Product Category Characteristics." *Journal of Marketing* 77 (4), 67–85

Kushwaha, Tarun, Venkatesh Shankar, and Shibo Li (2015), "The Store, the Web, and the Catalog Channels: Heterogeneous Customer Behavior and Resource Allocation." Chapel Hill, N.C.: University of North Carolina, Working Paper

Shankar, Venkatesh, and Tarun Kushwaha (2015), "Asymmetric Advertising and Cross-channel Effects: An Empirical Analysis." College Station, Tex.: Texas A&M University, Working Paper

Multichannel Customers: Product Category Risk

For low-risk categories, traditional channel customers provide greater monetary value than other channel customers. For utilitarian categories perceived as high risk, web-only customers provide the highest monetary value. For utilitarian categories perceived as low risk, catalog-only or store-only customers provide the highest monetary value.

Evidence base

Purchase and marketing information in a syndicated database of 96 million customers of 750 retailers across 22 product categories over a four-year period; transaction and marketing data across channels of over a million customers of a large shoe and accessory firm over a two-year period; attitudinal, behavioral, and marketing data of the insurance industry over a 42-month period

Managerial implications

1. Specialty retailers of low-risk products could induce traditional channel customers to spend more at their physical stores or through their catalogs by emphasizing items that are consistent with prevention focus. They could group similar products (e.g., surge protectors with cables and batteries, livestock feed with dog food and dog collars) through displays at the physical stores or in catalogs to remind prevention-focused customers to buy more items on each purchase occasion.

2. Specialty retailers of low-risk/utilitarian products could help traditional channel customers routinize their shopping and purchase more efficiently and repeatedly at their stores or through their catalogs. They could track the purchase histories of these customers and prompt them to buy more of the same items on a periodic basis.

3. Specialty retailers of high-risk/utilitarian products could make their websites sticky through features such as single-click ordering, product reviews, and new item recommendations. In this way, these retailers could make it convenient for promotion-focused customers who typically prefer the electronic channel to continue shopping and spend more in their preferred channel.

4. Specialty retailers of high-risk/utilitarian products could also educate their prevention-focused customers who prefer to shop through catalogs or at physical stores about the high trust levels at their web sites. In this way, they can help such customers reduce their risk perceptions and buy more from the web channel.

Contributors	Venkatesh Shankar, Texas A&M University, and Tarun Kushwaha, University of North Carolina at Chapel Hill
References	Kushwaha, Tarun, and Venkatesh Shankar (2013), "Are Multichannel Customers Really More Valuable? The Moderating Effects of Product Category Characteristics." *Journal of Marketing* 77 (4), 67–85
	Kushwaha, Tarun, Venkatesh Shankar, and Shibo Li (2015), "The Store, the Web, and the Catalog Channels: Heterogeneous Customer Behavior and Resource Allocation." Chapel Hill, N.C.: University of North Carolina, Working Paper
	Shankar, Venkatesh, and Tarun Kushwaha (2015), "Asymmetric Advertising and Cross-channel Effects: An Empirical Analysis." College Station, Tex.: Texas A&M University, Working Paper

14
Advertising

Advertising Elasticity

- The average short-term advertising elasticity is .12, which is substantially lower than the prior meta-analytic mean of .22 (Assmus, Farley, and Lehmann 1984).

- There has been a decline in the advertising elasticity over time; however, advertising elasticity is not significantly lower during economic recessions.

- Advertising elasticity is higher (1) for durable goods (.35) than nondurable goods (.11), (2) in the early stage of the life cycle (.16) than in the mature stage (.11), and (3) for yearly data (.26) than for quarterly data (.04).

- The mean long-term advertising elasticity is .24, which is much lower than the implied mean in the prior meta-analysis (.41).

- The omission of endogeneity induces a negative bias (underestimation) of the advertising elasticity.

Evidence base	Meta-analysis of 751 short-term and 402 long-term direct-to-consumer brand advertising elasticities estimated in 56 studies published between 1960 and 2008

Managerial implications	- The declining trend in advertising elasticity suggests a reduction in budgets allocated to conventional advertising, if firms were advertising optimally in the past. Alternately, a firm can take steps to increase advertising elasticity. - Advertising elasticity is not lower during recessions. So, at a minimum, managers need not reduce advertising in a recession because they erroneously believe that its sales impact will be lower than in expansion periods. - *Other things equal,* advertising should be higher for durable goods over non-durable goods and for products in the early stage of the life cycle over mature products. - Significant data interval differences underscore the need for determining and using the "right" data interval for estimating advertising elasticity. If data are available, less aggregate daily or weekly data may be better than quarterly or yearly data for obtaining unbiased estimates of advertising elasticity. - Advertising budgets may be endogenously determined by the firm, based on demand and response conditions. Where possible, such endogeneity should be taken into account in the modeling of advertising response and estimation of advertising elasticity.
Contributor	Raj Sethuraman, Southern Methodist University
References	Assmus, Gert, John U. Farley and Donald R. Lehmann (1984), "How Advertising Affects Sales: Meta-Analysis of Econometric Results." *Journal of Marketing Research* 21 (1), 65–74

Henningsen, Sina, Rebecca Heuke, and Michel Clement (2011), "Determinants of Advertising Effectiveness: The Development of an International Advertising Elasticity Database and a Meta-Analysis." *BuR–Business Research* 4 (2), 193–239

Sethuraman, Raj, Gerard Tellis, and Richard Briesch (2011), "How Well Does Advertising Work? Generalizations from Meta-Analysis of Brand Advertising Elasticities." *Journal of Marketing Research* 48 (3), 457–71

Long-term TV Advertising Impact

In cases where increased TV advertising has a significant impact on sales during the year of the weight increases, in the following two years, this sales impact is approximately doubled. On average, that doubling effect comes from an increase in buying rate in the test group. If TV advertising weight increases had no significant impact on sales during the first year, they had no impact in the two following years either.

Evidence base	55 TV advertising split cable tests which went on for three years where the only difference between test and control was the TV advertising treatment during the first year
Managerial implications	The impact of effective TV advertising is cumulative over at least a two-year period. However, if there is no significant effect in the short run, there is no significant effect in the long run. Thus, it is extremely profitable to find out whether TV advertising campaigns are working in the real world before putting big budgets behind them.
Contributor	Leonard M. Lodish, University of Pennsylvania
Reference	Lodish, Leonard M., Magid Abraham, Jeanne Livelsberger, Beth Lubetkin, Bruce Richardson, and Mary Ellen Stevens (1995), "A Summary of Fifty-five In-Market Experimental Estimates of the Long-Term Effect of TV Advertising." *Marketing Science* 14 (3) (Part 2 of 2), G133–40

Determinants of Advertising Impact

Advertising impact depends on the product category. Specifically, advertising elasticities are as much as 50% higher for durables as for non-durables. In addition, advertising is more effective for experience than for search products.

Evidence base	Review of more than 200 studies on advertising
Managerial implications	Brands competing in product-markets with high responsiveness to advertising should aggressively invest in advertising. Brands in markets with lower advertising effectiveness should carefully monitor their sales/advertising ratio and advertising ROI and invest more in other elements of the marketing mix.
Contributor	Demetrios Vakratsas, McGill University
References	Sethuraman, Raj, and Gerard J. Tellis (1991), "An Analysis of the Tradeoff Between Advertising and Price Discounting." *Journal of Marketing Research* 28 (2), 160–74
	Vakratsas, Demetrios, and Tim Ambler (1999), "How Advertising Works: What Do We Really Know?" *Journal of Marketing* 63 (1), 26–43

Advertising Impact and Competition

Higher competitive intensity (clutter) will result in lower advertising effectiveness. Competitive advertising may reduce elasticities by as much as 50%.

Evidence base	Multiple studies in packaged goods (e.g., personal care, detergents, ready-to-eat cereal) as well as durables (minivans, SUVs)
Managerial implications	Brands should overcome noise by advertising more heavily early on in the life cycle, when competitive intensity is lower, and "out-of-sync" with competitors, i.e., when their competitors do not advertise.
Contributor	Demetrios Vakratsas, McGill University
References	Danaher, Peter J., André Bonfrer, and Sanjay Dhar (2008), "The Effect of Competitive Advertising on Sales for Packaged Goods." *Journal of Marketing Research* 45 (2), 211–25
	Vakratsas, Demetrios, Fred M. Feinberg, Frank M. Bass, and Gurumurthy Kalyanaram (2004), "The Shape of Advertising Response Functions Revisited: A Model of Dynamic Probabilistic Thresholds." *Marketing Science* 23 (1), 109–19

Interference Effects of Competitive Advertising

Competitive advertising interference results in

1. attenuation in own-brand advertising elasticities, with elasticities in a cluttered environment being about half those observed when no competitors are advertising, and

2. a decline in sales as the proportion of competing brands that advertise increases (even for the same total quantity of competitive advertising). Moreover, having one more competitor advertise is generally more harmful to a focal brand's advertising effectiveness than if the present number of advertising brands increase their total ad volume.

Evidence base	Nine brands across the categories of liquid laundry detergent and ready-to-eat cereals for a major retailer in the Chicago area
Managerial implications	The widespread use of the budgeting rule "share-of-voice equals share-of-market" has resulted in an escalation of advertising spend in many product categories, thereby increasing ad clutter. Given that most advertisers today are operating in a cluttered environment, the effectiveness of their ads is reduced.
	However, if the clutter from competitive interference were lessened then advertising for the focal ad will have a chance to flourish. This means advertisers (especially for smaller brands) should avoid going head-to-head with competitors when scheduling their advertising. This can be achieved by choosing media or markets where there is less advertising from competitors. Also, particularly for television, advertisers could select particular days of the week to concentrate their advertising rather than spreading it over the week.

Contributors	Peter J. Danaher, Monash University, André Bonfrer, Australian National University, and Sanjay Dhar, University of Chicago
Reference	Danaher, P.J., André Bonfrer, and Sanjay Dhar (2008), "The Effect of Competitive Advertising Interference on Sales for Packaged Goods." *Journal of Marketing Research* 45 (April), 211–25

Advertising Weight

The size and distribution of media weight is an important determinant of advertising effectiveness. The bigger the change in the media weight and the more concentrated it is, the greater the advertising effectiveness.

Evidence base	Meta-analysis of 389 TV advertising experiments and review of 50 media scheduling studies
Managerial implications	Brands should opt for heavily concentrated media plans with big bumps rather than evenly distributed or standard flighted plans.
Contributor	Demetrios Vakratsas, McGill University
References	Lodish, Leonard M., Magid Abraham, Stuart Kalmenson, Jeanne Livelsberger, Beth Lubetkin, Bruce Richardson, and Mary Ellen Stevens (1995), "How T.V. Advertising Works: A Meta-Analysis of 389 Real World Split Cable T.V. Experiments." *Journal of Marketing Research* 32 (2), 125–39 Vakratsas, Demetrios, and Prasad Naik (2007), "Essentials of Planning Media Schedules." In *Handbook of Advertising*, eds. Gerard J. Tellis and Tim Ambler, 333–48. Los Angeles, Calif.: Sage Publications

Advertising Reference Price

The presence of an advertised reference in a price offer enhances consumers' internal reference price ($\eta = .26$) and their perceptions of value ($\eta = .21$) and lowers their intention to search for a lower price ($\eta = .17$). The level of the advertised reference in the price offer enhances consumers' internal reference price ($\eta = .29$) and their perceptions of value ($\eta = .25$) and lowers their intentions to search for a lower price ($\eta = .21$).

Evidence base	Meta-analysis of 38 studies
Managerial implications	As long as they adhere to "truth in advertising" and provide bona fide reference prices, managers should consider including them in ads, promotions, and displays, as these reference prices are likely to convey appropriate levels of value and will motivate purchase intent. However, at the same time, public policy makers need to carefully monitor the use of advertised reference prices as they have a strong potential to deceive consumers if these advertised reference prices are not bona fide prices.
Contributors	Dhruv Grewal, Babson College, and Larry D. Compeau, Clarkson University
References	Compeau, Larry D., and Dhruv Grewal (1998), "Comparative Price Advertising: An Integrative Review." *Journal of Public Policy and Marketing* 17 (Fall), 257–74
	Grewal, Dhruv, and Larry D. Compeau (1992), "Comparative Price Advertising: Informative or Deceptive?" *Journal of Public Policy and Marketing* 11 (Spring), 52–62

Comparative Advertising Impact

Comparative ads, relative to non-comparative ads, enhance message awareness, brand awareness, brand attitudes, intentions, and behaviors. These effects are stronger for new brands, leader comparison brands, and messages with higher credibility. Overall, comparative ads generate about 22% more purchases than non-comparative ads.

Evidence base	Meta-analysis of 77 studies
Managerial implications	Comparative advertising is a common method, in which the sponsored firm or brand compares its product or service against some comparison brand. The results highlight that this method is very effective for enhancing brand attitudes and purchase behavior; it is most effective when the sponsored brand's position is lower than the comparison brand's and when the advertising message has high credibility.
Contributor	Dhruv Grewal, Babson College
Reference	Grewal, Dhruv, Sukumar Kavanoor, Edward F. Fern, Carolyn Costley, and James Barnes (1997), "Comparative Versus Noncomparative Advertising: A Meta-Analysis." *Journal of Marketing* 61 (October), 1–15

Advertising Impact Duration

The average advertising duration interval on sales is brief—typically between six and nine months.

Evidence base	Aggregation-bias-adjusted results from meta-analysis findings by Clarke (1976) across 70 studies and Assmus, Farley, and Lehmann (1984) across 128 models from 22 studies
Managerial implications	Managers should not expect that the tangible impact of their advertising lasts for years. In most cases it lasts less than three business quarters. Researchers should be aware of data aggregation bias, i.e., the longer the data interval (e.g., quarterly as compared to weekly), the longer the advertising effect appears to last.
Contributor	Robert P. Leone, Texas Christian University
References	Assmus, Gert, John U. Farley, and Donald R. Lehmann (1984), "How Advertising Affects Sales: Meta-Analysis of Econometric Results." *Journal of Marketing Research* 21 (1), 65–74
	Bass, Frank M., and Robert P. Leone (1983), "Temporal Aggregation, the Data Interval Bias, and Empirical Estimation of Bimonthly Relations from Annual Data." *Management Science* 29 (1), 1–11
	Clarke, D. G. (1976), "Econometric Measurement of the Duration of Advertising Effect on Sales." *Journal of Marketing Research* 13 (November), 345–57
	Leone, Robert P. (1995), "Generalizing What Is Known About Temporal Aggregation and Advertising Carryover." *Marketing Science* 14 (3) (Part 2 of 2), G141–50

TV Advertising Effect

The average TV advertising to sales elasticity is .11 for established consumer products. It is higher for tests after 1995 than those before. There is a high variability in effects around these average elasticities. Some tests had elasticities over .5 and others were below −.05.

Evidence base	241 real-world TV advertising tests conducted by Information Resources, Inc. from 1989 to 2003
Managerial implications	To increase brand profits, it pays to test TV advertising in market prior to running it, thus only running TV campaigns that are generating returns higher than their costs.
Contributor	Leonard M. Lodish, University of Pennsylvania
References	Hu, Ye, Leonard M. Lodish, and Abba M. Krieger (2007), "An Analysis of Real World TV Advertising Tests: A 15-Year Update." *Journal of Advertising Research* 47 (3), 341–53
	Lodish, Leonard M., Magid Abraham, Stuart Kalmenson, Jeanne Livelsberger, Beth Lubetkin, Bruce Richardson, and Mary Ellen Stevens (1995), "How T.V. Advertising Works: A Meta-Analysis of 389 Real World Split Cable T.V. Experiments." *Journal of Marketing Research* 32 (2), 125–39

Ownership of Digital Video Recorders and TV Advertising Impact

The average (across categories) annual household-level change in advertised brand sales for households who received a DVR (relative to those who did not) was just .02 cents in the first year and another −.02 cents in the second year. The standard errors of these effects are .3 cents, meaning the differences are not statistically significant. These null effects persist even one or two years after the adoption of the DVR. They also hold for private label sales and for the growth of new brands.

Evidence base	48 different consumer packaged goods product categories in four IRI U.S. markets.
Managerial implications	DVR ownership does not affect sales. Several potential explanations exist for the lack of a DVR effect: (1) advertising has no effect on sales so a DVR has no effect on sales, (2) fast-forwarded ads are still effective exposures, and (3) the fraction of advertising avoidance is not extensive (around 6.5% in the study).
Contributors	Bart J. Bronnenberg, Tilburg University, Jean-Pierre Dubé, University of Chicago, and Carl F. Mela, Duke University
Reference	Bronnenberg, Bart, Jean-Pierre Dubé, and Carl F. Mela (2010), "Do Digital Video Recorders Influence Sales?" *Journal of Marketing Research* 47 (6), 998–1010

Effects of Ad-evoked Feelings on Brand Attitudes

TV ad-evoked feelings have a substantial impact on consumers' attitudes toward the advertised brand, with a correlation between ad-evoked feelings and brand evaluations of $r = .33$. This effect does not depend on the level of involvement associated with the product category but is slightly more pronounced for hedonic products than utilitarian products.

Evidence base	Analysis of 1,576 consumers' responses to 1,070 TV commercials from more than 150 different product categories
Managerial implications	All advertisers benefit from ads that evoke pleasant emotional feelings, with marketers of hedonic products benefiting slightly more than marketers of utilitarian products. Advertisers should not ignore the importance of ad-evoked feelings even if they market high-involvement products.
Contributor	Michel Tuan Pham, Columbia University
Reference	Michel Tuan Pham, Maggie Geuens, and Patrick De Pelsmaker (2013), "The Influence of Ad-Evoked Feelings on Brand Evaluations: Empirical Generalizations from Consumer Responses to More Than 1,000 TV Commercials." *International Journal of Research in Marketing* 30 (4), 383–94

TV Advertising and Online Search and Shopping

Television advertising produces a variety of effects on Internet shopping behavior. TV ads can stimulate product category search; increase the usage of branded keywords in place of generic keywords; stimulate or depress direct traffic to the brand website; and stimulate immediate shopping and sales on the brand's website. Television advertising content that encourages direct action increases immediate direct website traffic and sales.

Evidence base	Changes in Internet shopping and sales in narrow windows of time around the airing of 350,000 TV ad insertions worth $3.4 billion by 20 brands in four product categories; hourly analysis of Google search data and $1.7 billion spent on TV advertising by 24 financial services brands over three months; second-by-second analysis of server logs and a large-scale TV ad experiment for an anonymous brand
Managerial implications	Advertisers must consider how television advertising affects multitaskers' behavior online. ROI metrics that fail to account for traditional media's brand-building effects will likely lead marketers to spend too little on TV and too much on digital. Traditional and digital agencies should work together to plan, execute, evaluate, and integrate their marketing communications.
Contributor	Kenneth C. Wilbur, University of California, San Diego
References	Joo, M., K.C. Wilbur, B. Cowgill, and Y. Zhu (2014), "Television Advertising and Online Search." *Management Science* 60 (1), 56–73

Kitts, Brendan, et al. (2014) "Can Television Advertising Impact Be Measured on the Web? Web Spike Response as a Possible Conversion Tracking System for Television." *Proceedings of 20th ACM SIGKDD Conference on Knowledge Discovery and Data Mining.* ACM, New York City.

Liaukonyte, J., T. Teixeira, and Kenneth C. Wilbur (2015), "Television Advertising and Online Shopping." *Marketing Science* 34 (3), 311–30

Zigmond, Dan, and Horst Stipp (2010) "Assessing a New Advertising Effect: Measurement of the Impact of Television Commercials on Internet Search Queries." *Journal of Advertising Research* 50 (2), 162–8

Zigmond, Dan, and Horst Stipp (2011), "Multitaskers May Be Advertisers' Best Audience." *Harvard Business Review* 12 (1/2), 32–3

Advertising and Sports Events

Own advertising–sales elasticities are much smaller around major sports events compared to normal periods. Decreases in effectiveness amount to 75% for short-term elasticities and 45% for long-term elasticities. Reductions are strongest right before and during the event, and weakest right after the event. Cross-advertising elasticities are reduced as well.

Brands can escape from these reductions when they (1) invest heavily in advertising, resulting in higher share of voice (2) around events that focus on one sport. For such brands, long-term elasticities even increase by approximately 50% right after the event.

Evidence base	Time-series analysis of four years of weekly data on 206 brands across 64 consumer packaged goods categories in the U.K. (2002–2005); focus on sales effects of "normal" advertising
Managerial implications	If brands have sufficient budgets, it pays off to invest heavily in advertising, and increase share of voice around single-sport events in order to increase sales. If such funds are not available, brands should try to escape from the clutter. They can (1) shift their budgets to other marketing tools, or (2) concentrate advertising efforts on the weeks right after the event. Investing in advertising around these events can still make sense when advertising is used as catalyst of other marketing activities or to build brand image.
Contributor	Maarten J. Gijsenberg, University of Groningen
Reference	Gijsenberg, Maarten J. (2014), "Going for Gold: Investigating the (Non)Sense of Increased Advertising around Major Sports Events." *International Journal of Research in Marketing* 31 (1), 2–15

Pharmaceutical Promotional Expenditures

Promotional and advertising expenditures have a significant and positive effect on sales in pharmaceutical markets. The elasticities differ considerably between marketing instruments: the effect of detailing is largest (average elasticity = .326), followed by direct-to-practitioner (DTP) advertising (average elasticity = .123), direct-to-consumer advertising (average elasticity = .073), and other DTP instruments (average elasticity = .062).

Evidence base	Meta-analysis of 58 empirical studies, reporting 781 promotional elasticities in pharmaceutical markets
Managerial implications	Promotional expenditures stimulate the sales of pharmaceuticals, but their effectiveness depends on several factors, including the promotional instruments used and the disease category. The moderate effects of promotional expenditures should interest policy makers, who may be overestimating the role of marketing efforts in the sector.
Contributor	Tammo Bijmolt, University of Groningen
Reference	Kremer, Sara T.M., Tammo H.A. Bijmolt, Peter S.H. Leeflang, and Jaap E. Wieringa (2008), "Generalizations on the Effectiveness of Pharmaceutical Expenditures." *International Journal of Research in Marketing* 25 (4), 234–46

Advertising and Cigarette Consumption

The weighted average effect size for cigarette advertising and the initiation of smoking is .087. For the continuation of smoking the effect size is .007, and for brand switching the effect size is .131. Factors that enhance the effect of cigarette advertising are whether or not the consumer was an adult, and whether or not the advertising took place outside the U.S.

Evidence base	Comprehensive meta-analytical review incorporating 52 studies and 118 weighted estimates
Managerial implications	Advertising is salient in a consumer's decision to begin cigarette smoking. Advertising is also related to a consumer's decision to continue smoking. Advertising has its strongest impact on brand switching (loyalty) and weakest on continuation (which may largely be driven by physical addiction). Cigarette advertising is a significant predictor of cigarette brand loyalty and brand switching behavior, but has a minor impact on total product category sales. The relation of advertising to cigarette consumption is greater for adults than for adolescents. Cigarette advertising in markets outside the U.S. is more impactful.
Contributor	Michael L. Capella, Villanova University
Reference	Capella, Michael L., Cynthia Webster, and Brian R. Kinard (2011), "A Review of the Effect of Cigarette Advertising." *International Journal of Research in Marketing* 28 (3), 269–79

Product Placement Effectiveness

Product placements in motion pictures generate positive financial returns (.75% stock price bump on average). However, the effects of these product placements, as well as tie-in advertising campaigns, have declined since their peak effects in the 1990s.

There are diminishing returns to brand appearances on the screen: for every additional appearance with the main character, the cumulative abnormal return (CAR) for a given stock decreased by .42%.

Placements in movies with romantic themes resulted in drastically lower returns, which could result in negative returns. Placements in dramas resulted in marginally lower returns compared to non-drama movies.

Evidence base	Event study of 928 product placements in 159 films released over four decades
Managerial implications	Qualification of where to place products is becoming more important, as the returns from generic placements have declined over time. Preexisting placement agreements can signal suitability of the project because total number of products placed was not found to impact performance. Subtle placements in the background may not only be less costly, but also more effective.
Contributors	Ekaterina V. Karniouchina, Mills College, and Can Uslay, Rutgers University
Reference	Karniouchina, Ekaterina V., Can Uslay, and Grigori Erenburg (2011), "Do Marketing Media Have Life Cycles? The Case of Product Placement in Movies." *Journal of Marketing* 75 (May), 27–48

Search Engine Advertising and Bidding Heuristics

In search engine advertising, prices per click and clickthrough rates (CTRs) increase with better ranks. The rate at which they increase is the strongest for branded keywords (often higher than 100% increase), and the lowest for generic keywords (typically around 50%). The percentage increases in prices per click and clickthrough rates are often very closely aligned.

Evidence base	Empirical study of percentage increases in four different industries (fashion, mobile phones, industrial goods, travel) with 30 keywords each; empirical study of 310 keywords (13 generic, 85 branded, and 23 retailer keywords) from nine different industries (airlines, automotive, banking, online banking, drug stores, energy, telecommunications, travel, insurance)
Managerial implications	If data are lacking to determine an optimal bid (because of missing values in the data or because a campaign was newly set-up), advertisers can use a simple heuristic for bidding, which equals 50% of their profit per click.
Contributors	Nadia Abou Nabout, Vienna University of Economics and Business, and Bernd Skiera, Goethe University Frankfurt
References	Abou Nabout, Nadia, Bernd Skiera, T. Stepanchuk, and E. Gerstmeier (2012), "An Analysis of the Profitability of Fee-Based Compensation Plans for Search Engine Marketing." *International Journal of Research in Marketing* 29 (1), 68–80 Abou Nabout, Nadia (2015), "A Novel Approach for Bidding on Keywords in Newly Set-up Search Advertising Campaigns." *European Journal of Marketing* 49 (5/6), 668–91

Ghose, Anindya, and S. Yang (2009), "An Empirical Analysis of Search Engine Advertising: Sponsored Search in Electronic Markets." *Management Science* 55 (10), 1605–22

Skiera, Bernd, and Nadia Abou Nabout (2013), "PROSAD: A Bidding Decision Support System for Profit Optimizing Search Engine Advertising." *Marketing Science* 32 (2), 213–20

Search Engine Advertising Prices

In search engine advertising, prices per click are highest in the United States and United Kingdom, as well as in the financial and Internet services industries. They are lower in retail than in services industries. Over time, prices paid per click have significantly increased from $2.06 in April 2009 to $2.72 in November 2012.

Evidence base	Empirical study at eight different points in time between 2009 and 2012, in six countries, 15 industries per country, and five keywords per industry and country
Managerial implications	Between 2009 and 2012, prices of search engine advertising increased much more than the inflation rate. Budget increases for search engine advertising may increase prices per click but not the number of clicks (advertising effectiveness). Advertisers thus need to be careful when using higher budgets to submit higher bids because of bidding wars that may ultimately increase prices per click, but not advertising effectiveness.
Contributors	Nadia Abou Nabout, Vienna University of Economics and Business, and Bernd Skiera, Goethe University Frankfurt
Reference	Abou Nabout, Nadia, Markus Lilienthal, and Bernd Skiera (2014), "Empirical Generalizations in Search Engine Advertising." *Journal of Retailing* 90 (2), 206–16

Advertising and Firm Value

The mean firm-value elasticity with respect to advertising expenditures is .04, while the mean firm-value elasticity with respect to marketing-asset variables (including brand and customer relationship) is .54. The elasticities are smaller when firm value is measured as stock returns, as opposed to market capitalization.

Evidence base	Meta-analysis based on 488 elasticities drawn from 83 studies
Managerial implications	Given that the vast majority of marketing firm-value elasticities is positive, investing in marketing is value-relevant. The potential for growing firm value is especially large with respect to marketing assets. The results suggest that firms are still underinvested in brands and customer relationships, since the firm-value elasticities should be zero at optimal investment levels.
Contributors	Marc Fischer, University of Cologne and University of Technology, Sydney, and Alexander Edeling, University of Cologne
Reference	Edeling, Alexander, and Marc Fischer (2014), "Marketing's Impact on Firm Value: Generalizations from a Meta-Analysis." Cambridge, Mass.: Marketing Science Institute, Report No. 14–107

15

Marketing Mix

Household Response to Marketing

Sensitivity to marketing mix variables is predominantly a consumer trait and is not unique to specific product categories. In particular, higher-income households are less price sensitive and large families are more price sensitive. Households that visit the store often are more price sensitive. Households with larger market baskets are less price sensitive. Heavy-user households tend to be both less price sensitive and less display sensitive.

Evidence base	Consumer products: Bayesian multi-category model on panel data on five categories and 300 households
Managerial implications	Many firms offer multiple product categories. Given consumer types (bargain hunters, status conscious, etc.) that respond similarly across elements of the marketing mix, many aspects of such firms' marketing efforts can be common across the different product categories.
Contributor	Andrew Ainslie, University of Rochester
Reference	Ainslie, Andrew, and Peter E. Rossi (1998), "Similarities in Choice Behavior across Product Categories." *Marketing Science* 17 (2), 91–106

Decomposition of Long-term Effects of Marketing Actions

Only 20% of the net sales effect of a marketing action is due to the initial campaign itself; most of the remaining effect stems from the synergy with other marketing actions (in the case of strategic actions such as new products and advertising) or from inertia (in the case of tactical actions such as price and feature).

Evidence base	Across 81 brands in 26 fast-moving consumer product categories
Managerial implications	Consumer reaction to the initial marketing action matters, but the net long-term effect is largely driven by company decisions to prolong the action and/or to support it with other marketing activities. Managers need to be aware of and attempt to capture such synergies in assessing the ROI of specific elements of (and the overall) marketing mix.
Contributor	Koen Pauwels, Özyeğin University
References	Pauwels, Koen (2004), "How Dynamic Consumer Response, Competitor Response, Company Support and Company Inertia Shape Long-Term Marketing Effectiveness." *Marketing Science* 23 (4), 596–610
	Pauwels, Koen (2007), "How Retailer and Competitor Decisions Drive the Long-Term Effectiveness of Manufacturer Promotions for Fast Moving Consumer Goods." *Journal of Retailing* 83 (3), 297–308

Mindset Metrics

Mindset metrics of awareness, consideration, and liking impact sales above and beyond the direct effect of advertising, price, distribution, and promotions on sales. Own and competitive mindset metrics account for about 16% of the variation in brand sales.

Evidence base	Analysis of over 74 brands in four categories over a seven-year period in France
Managerial implications	Building share in the customer's "mind and heart" translates into improved marketplace performance. Mindset metrics lead sales by several months, allowing time for managerial action before market performance itself is affected. When possible, mindset metrics should be included in sales response models.
Contributor	Shuba Srinivasan, Boston University
Reference	Srinivasan, Shuba, Marc Vanhuele, and Koen Pauwels (2008), "Do Mindset Metrics Explain Brand Sales?" Cambridge, Mass.: Marketing Science Institute, Report No. 08–119

Marketing/Sales Ratios

Marketing expenditures typically range between 10% and 20% of sales revenue. The ratios are highest for businesses with high gross profit margins. Sales force/sales ratios average three times advertising/sales ratios. Business-to-business (B-to-B) typically spend five to six times as much on sales force budgets as advertising, while spending only about half as much on total marketing as a percentage of sales as do business-to-consumer (B-to-C) businesses. Both B-to-B and B-to-C spend more on marketing/sales when selling new products, products purchased in low dollar amounts, and more frequently purchased products. These generalizations are also consistent with meta-analyses of marginal elasticities for sales force and advertising spending.

Evidence base	Empirical studies of data from ADVISOR, PIMS, and COMPUSTAT
Managerial implications	These generalizations of marketing cost ratios provide broad benchmarks for spending, that is, what a firm "like yours" would most likely spend in a market like yours. These can be refined by experimental and econometric studies of response functions. Further, the generalizations can help project what changes in marketing spending are most likely to occur when market, competitive, or environmental conditions change.
Contributors	Paul Farris, University of Virginia, and Gary L. Lilien, Pennsylvania State University
References	Farris, Paul W., and Robert D. Buzzell (1979), "Why Advertising and Promotion Costs Vary: Some Cross Sectional Analyses." *Journal of Marketing* 43 (4), 112–22

Lilien, Gary L. (1979), "ADVISOR 2: Modeling the Marketing Mix Decision for Industrial Products." *Management Science* 25 (2), 191–204

Lilien, Gary L., and David Weinstein (1984), "An International Comparison of the Determinants of Industrial Marketing Expenditures." *Journal of Marketing* 48 (1), 46–53

Reibstein, David J., Yogesh Joshi, and Paul W. Farris (2004), "Marketing Costs and Prices." In *The Profit Impact of Marketing Strategy Project: Retrospect and Prospects*, eds. Paul W. Farris and Michael J. Moore, 124–52. New York, N.Y.: Cambridge University Press

Post-launch Strategy and New-brand Performance

Among several elements of the marketing mix (pricing, discounting, feature and display, product-line length, distribution depth and breadth, and advertising), *distribution breadth* explains 54% of the observed variation in the market potential for new brands. The effects of the other elements are small relative to that of distribution.

Evidence base	Analysis of 225 new consumer brand launches in France
Managerial implications	As long as the *incremental* cost of obtaining additional distribution breadth (ACV, all commodity volume) is less than 24% of retail sales, it is profitable to invest in distribution. The comparable figure for advertising is 1% of sales.
Contributor	Carl F. Mela, Duke University
Reference	Ataman, M. Berk, Carl F. Mela, and Harald J. van Heerde (2008), "Building Brands." *Marketing Science* 27 (6), 1036–54

Long-term Effect of Marketing Strategy on Brand Sales

The long-term unit sales elasticity is 1.29 for product line length and .61 for distributional penetration. In contrast, the long-term elasticity for advertising is .12 and the long-run elasticity for price discounting is negative: −.04. In sum, new products and broader distribution have a greater long-term effect on sales than increases in advertising and price promotions.

The short-term price elasticity increases with discounting and broader distribution, as better retail availability makes it easier for consumers to price shop, while discounts train consumers to buy on deal. In contrast, the short-term price elasticity is reduced when brands advertise more and when they offer a broader product line.

Evidence base	70 mature French consumer-packaged goods brands across 25 categories and five years
Managerial implications	For mature CPG brands, product line development has the strongest effect on brand sales in the long run. Moreover, longer product lines lower price sensitivity, thereby enabling firms to maintain pricing power. Distribution is another effective way to enhance sales in the long run.
	Compared to product line length and distribution, advertising has a relatively weak long-term effect on sales, though it also lowers price sensitivity. Though discounting plays a largely tactical role by generating strong sales increases in the short run, it has an adverse effect in the long term owing to diminished future sales and heightened price sensitivity.

Contributors	Harald J. van Heerde, Massey University, Carl. F. Mela, Duke University, and Berk Ataman, Koç University
Reference	Ataman, Berk, Harald J. van Heerde, and Carl. F. Mela (2010), "The Long-term Effect of Marketing Strategy on Brand Sales." *Journal of Marketing Research* 47 (5), 866–82

Demand and Supply Dynamics for Motion Pictures

In the release week, the demand for a movie is strongly driven by its quality (elasticity: 1.05) and its distribution (numbers of screens; elasticity: 1.04). In later stages, the influence of the distribution on demand remains very high (elasticity: 1.00) and is accompanied by a high impact of word-of-mouth (elasticity: .85). Demand expectations play a major role for screen allocation (elasticity: .40 for the first week). Advertising drives the supply of screens (elasticity: .30), with larger effects measured for the U.S.

Evidence base	2,098 motion pictures released in the U.S. (2000–2010); 1,360 motion pictures released in Germany (2002–2010)
Managerial implications	Aside from content-specific factors driving the quality of the movie, the major managerial challenge for studios and distributors is to generate distribution power and manage word-of-mouth. While the demand effects of advertising and production budget are limited, they have strong *signaling power* to the suppliers of screens.
	Movie executives should appreciate that the entire marketing mix is important for promoting a new movie. The effectiveness of their marketing actions differs for moviegoers and movie theaters (exhibitors).
Contributors	Michel Clement and Steven Wu, University of Hamburg, and Marc Fischer, University of Cologne and University of Technology, Sydney

Reference   Clement, Michel, Steven Wu, and Marc Fischer (2014), "Empirical Generalizations of Demand and Supply Dynamics for Movies." *International Journal of Research in Marketing* 31 (2), 207–23

Executive Compensation, Advertising and R&D Spending and Stock Returns

An increase in the ratio of longer term equity-based compensation relative to short-term performance-based bonus is positively associated with an increase in advertising and R&D spending as a share of sales. This effect is larger for smaller firms, but does not meaningfully vary across industries. In addition, advertising and R&D spending mediate the effect of equity-to-bonus ratio on stock market return, i.e., compensation affects spending which, in turn, affects stock returns.

Evidence base	ExecuComp, COMPUSTAT, and CRSP data on 842 firms from 1993 to 2005
Managerial implications	If a firm has strategic interests in value creation, through continuous investments in R&D for new product and process development, and in value appropriation, through continuous investments in advertising for building brands and sales, there should be a clear recognition among members of the compensation committee that top executives have a powerful short-term disincentive to spend on advertising and R&D. Increasing the equity-to-bonus ratio incentivizes top executives to achieve not just desired long-term goals for investments but stock market return as well.
Contributors	Imran S. Currim, University of California at Irvine, and Jooseop Lim, Concordia University
Reference	Currim, Imran S., Jooseop Lim, and Joung W. Kim (2012), "You Get What You Pay For: The Effect of Top Executives' Compensation on Advertising and R&D Spending Decisions and Stock Market Return." *Journal of Marketing* 76 (5), 33–48

16

Competitive Reaction

Competitive Reaction

The predominant form of competitive reaction to advertising and promotion attacks is to do nothing. For 54% of the brands under price promotion attack, there is no short-run promotion reaction, and 85% of these brands do not react with advertising changes. By the same token, 82% of the brands under advertising attack do not react with advertising and 68% do not react with promotion. Long-run reactions happen even less often—occurring in less than 10% of the cases.

Evidence base	Analysis of reaction patterns for over 1,200 brands in 442 packaged goods categories covering four years of weekly scanner data in the Netherlands
Managerial implications	From a sales maximization point of view, most of the observed brands are justified in their decision not to react (88% of promotion cases and virtually all advertising instances). Managers should carefully consider alternatives before automatically responding in kind to competitors' promotions or advertising.
Contributors	Jan-Benedict E.M. Steenkamp, University of North Carolina at Chapel Hill, and Marnik G. Dekimpe, Tilburg University and Catholic University of Leuven

Reference Steenkamp, Jan-Benedict E.M., Vincent R. Nijs, Dominique M. Hanssens, and Marnik G. Dekimpe (2005), "Competitive Reactions to Advertising and Promotion Attacks." *Marketing Science* 24 (1), 35–54

About the Editor

Dominique M. Hanssens is the Bud Knapp Distinguished Professor of Marketing at the UCLA Anderson School of Management. From 2005 to 2007 he served as Executive Director of the Marketing Science Institute.

A Purdue University Ph.D. graduate, Hanssens' research focuses on strategic marketing problems, in particular marketing productivity, to which he applies his expertise in data-analytic methods such as econometrics and time-series analysis. He has served or is serving in various editorial capacities with *Marketing Science, Management Science, Journal of Marketing Research,* and *International Journal of Research in Marketing*. Five of his articles have won Best Paper awards, in *Marketing Science* (1995, 2001, 2002), *Journal of Marketing Research* (1999, 2007) and *Journal of Marketing* (2010), and eight were award finalists. The second edition of his book with Leonard Parsons and Randall Schultz, entitled *Market Response Models,* was published in 2001 and has been translated in Chinese and Japanese.

He is a Fellow of the INFORMS Society for Marketing Science (ISMS) and the 2015 recipient of the ISMS Buck Weaver Award. He is also a recipient of the Churchill and Mahajan Lifetime Achievement awards from the American Marketing Association. He is a founding partner of MarketShare, a global marketing analytics firm headquartered in Los Angeles.

About the Marketing Science Institute

Founded in 1961, the Marketing Science Institute is a nonprofit, membership-based organization dedicated to bridging the gap between academic marketing theory and business practice. MSI is unique as the only research-based organization with an expansive network of practically-minded marketing academics from the best business schools all over the world as well as thoughtful practitioners from 70+ leading companies.

The MSI mission is to bring the best of science to the complex world of marketing. Through high-quality events and activities, cutting-edge content and publications, and productive networking opportunities, MSI members stay on the forefront of marketing thought and practice. MSI is an indispensable means to enhance professional development and improve marketing decision making for each of its members and member organizations.